Rousseau, Law and the Sovereignty of the People

Together with Plato's *Republic,* Jean-Jacques Rousseau's *Social Contract* is regarded as one of the most original examples of utopian political engineering in the history of ideas. Similar to the *Republic,* Rousseau's masterwork is better known today for its author's idiosyncratic view of political justice than its lessons on lawmaking or governance in any concrete sense. Challenging this common view, *Rousseau, Law and the Sovereignty of the People* examines the Genevan's contributions as a legislator and builder of institutions, relating his major ideas to issues and debates in twenty-first century political science. Ethan Putterman explores how Rousseau's just state would actually operate, investigating how laws would be drafted, ratified and executed, arguing that the theory of the *Social Contract* is more pragmatic and populist than many scholars assume today.

ETHAN PUTTERMAN is Assistant Professor at the Department of Political Science, National University of Singapore. He is a past Fellow in the Society for the Liberal Arts in the College at the University of Chicago.

Rousseau, Law and the Sovereignty of the People

ETHAN PUTTERMAN

CAMBRIDGE
UNIVERSITY PRESS

CAMBRIDGE UNIVERSITY PRESS
Cambridge, New York, Melbourne, Madrid, Cape Town, Singapore,
São Paulo, Delhi, Dubai, Tokyo

Cambridge University Press
The Edinburgh Building, Cambridge CB2 8RU, UK

Published in the United States of America by Cambridge University Press,
New York

www.cambridge.org
Information on this title: www.cambridge.org/9780521765381

First published 2010

Printed in the United Kingdom at the University Press, Cambridge

A catalog record for this publication is available from the British Library

Library of Congress Cataloging in Publication data
Putterman, Ethan.
Rousseau, law, and the sovereignty of the people / Ethan Putterman.
    p.   cm.
ISBN 978-0-521-76538-1 (hardback)
1. Rousseau, Jean-Jacques, 1712–1778.   2. Social contract.   3. Law–Political
aspects–Philosophy.   I. Title.
K457.R6P88 2010
340′.11–dc22
2010000060

ISBN 978-0-521-76538-1 Hardback

To Iris

It is to law alone that men owe justice and freedom. It is this healthy instrument of the will of all that reestablishes, as a right, the natural equality among men. It is this celestial voice that tells each citizen the precepts of public reason, and teaches him to act according to the maxims of his own judgment and not to be in contradiction with himself.

Discourse on Political Economy, 1755

Contents

Acknowledgments

I am grateful to the National University of Singapore and the University of Chicago for financial support during the writing of this book. I would like to thank the University Press of New England for permission to cite extensively from the excellent translations of Rousseau's works in the *Collected Writings of Rousseau* (volumes 1–12). This extraordinary collection of translations is an invaluable resource to Rousseau scholars around the world. In addition, I wish to thank the editors and publishers of the *American Political Science Review* and *Political Studies* for permission to reprint the revised drafts of articles that appear in Chapters 2 and 5. The original versions of these articles appeared in *APSR*, 97:3 (August 2003) with a subsequent debate with John T. Scott in *APSR*, 99 (February 2005) and *Political Studies*, 49:3 (August 2001).

At the outset, I wish to thank Tracy B. Strong and John P. McCormick for providing thoughtful and lengthy comments to the manuscript for this book. Their respective contributions are especially evident in my discussion of the laws and Rome in Chapters 1 and 3. I am also grateful to Roger D. Masters for a critical reading of an early draft of Chapter 6 (as an unpublished APSA paper). I regard Professor Masters as the standard-bearer on the topic of Rousseau's political philosophy in the world today. I also wish to thank John Haslam at Cambridge University Press and Sarah Price and Gail Welsh at Out of House Publishing Solutions, Ltd.

During my academic life I have benefited enormously from the teachings of an exemplary roster of distinguished professors. This was never more so than during my graduate years as a student in the Department of Political Science at the University of Chicago. The person to whom I am most indebted from this time is Bernard

Manin. This book would have been inconceivable without his invaluable guidance and encouragement over many years. Bernard is a true mentor and friend. I am also indebted to Robert Morrissey, William Sewell and François Furet. Much of what I know about the intellectual history of the French Revolution I learned from Professor Furet.

I also want to thank four exemplary educators whose involvement in my professional and personal life extended far beyond the classroom: Marvin Zonis, Moishe Postone, Terry Nardin and Dr Anne Bohm of the London School of Economics. At critical stages of my academic career the concerned involvement of each of these four individuals was instrumental to my remaining within the profession. It is indeed true that some debts can never be repaid. For different reasons, I also wish to thank Jon Elster, Alexander Kaufman, Cameron M. Burns, Brad Williams, Kyaw Yin Hlaing, Lee Lai To, Constantin Fasolt, Nathan Tarcov, Mads Qvortrup, and Ed Mensa.

More than anybody else the person to whom I owe the greatest debt for becoming a political theorist is David Mapel of the University of Colorado at Boulder. Together with David Gross in the Department of History both scholars inspired my early love of political philosophy.

Lastly, and most importantly, I wish to thank my family, Josh Putterman, Suzanne Gordon, Scott Webster, Walden Putterman, Talia Putterman, Maurice and Rachel Elkabas and – most of all – my parents, Carol Adams and Alan Putterman for everything that each has given me over many years. This book is dedicated to my wife, Iris Putterman.

A note on the text

The page numbers and citations from Rousseau's writings in this book refer to:

1 the *Collected Writings of Rousseau*, vols. 1–10, University Press of New England, ed. Christopher Kelly and Roger D. Masters (1990, 1992, 1992, 1994, 1995, 1997, 1998, 2000, 2001, 2003, 2005); and
2 the standard five-volume Gallimard edition of the *Oeuvres Complètes*, ed. Robert Dérathe and Bernard Gagnebin (1959, 1964, 1964, 1969, 1995).

All other references to Rousseau's writings not found in these collected editions refer to the translations listed in the bibliography.

Abbreviations

C	*Confessions*
CGP	*Considerations on the Government of Poland*
CS	*Social Contract*
DI	*Discourse on Inequality Among Men*
DSA	*Discourse on the Arts and Sciences*
DV	*Discourse on the Virtue Most Necessary for a Hero*
E	*Emile*
EOL	*Essay on the Origin of Languages*
EP	*Discourse on Political Economy*
FP	*Political Fragments*
JNH	*Julie or the New Eloise*
LA	*Letter to M. Alembert*
LCB	*Letter to Christopher Beaumont*
LEM	*Letters Written from the Mountain*
LV	*Letter to Voltaire*
MG	*Geneva Manuscript*
ML	*Moral Letters*
N	*Narcissus, or the Lover of Himself*
PC	*Project for Corsica*
RJJ	*Rousseau: Judge of Jean Jacques*
RPS	*Reveries of the Solitary Walker*

Introduction: The celestial voice

Few works of political philosophy are as famous or familiar as Jean-Jacques Rousseau's *Social Contract*. One of the most celebrated and complex of the great masterworks of the Western canon, Rousseau's diminutive treatise on statecraft has been the subject of extended studies and short primers on political philosophy for over two and a half centuries. First published in Amsterdam and Paris in 1762 as part of a broader study of political institutions, the *Social Contract* remains the most original and, arguably, radical defense of participatory democracy in the whole history of political thought. As one scholar comments, it is a groundbreaking work penned by a thinker who, more than anybody else, ought to be regarded as the "theorist *par excellence* of participation."[1]

Widely heralded as a brilliant yet gratuitously utopian book, this most well-known of Rousseau's writings is also considered to be his most fanciful: a fantastically idealistic treatise on the nature of legitimate government intended for an audience in which "the awful distance between the possible and the probable" is knowingly unbridgeable.[2] According to many readers, the political program of the *Social Contract* was always intended to be a work on the abstract principles of political obligation and never a manual on practical or feasible institutions in any concrete sense. As Jean Guéhenno commented some time ago, Rousseau was a political romantic who was "carried away by his dreams," sketching down his imaginings

---

[1] Carole Pateman, *Participation and Democratic Theory*, Cambridge: Cambridge University Press, 1970, 22.
[2] Judith N. Shklar, *Men and Citizens: A Study of Rousseau's Social Theory*, Cambridge and New York: Cambridge University Press, 1987 [1969], 2.

"with all the fanaticism of a priest and the fantasy of a backyard inventor."[3]

This judgment echoes that of a chorus of commentators dating back to Benjamin Constant and Edmund Burke who, two centuries earlier, characterized the Genevan's political theory as being, on the whole, "so inapplicable to real life" that "we never dream of drawing from them any rule for laws or conduct."[4] This early description, which seats Rousseau near the head of a long table of utopian dreamers stretching back to Thomas More and Plato, was voiced by many Anglo-American thinkers at the end of the eighteenth century and, afterward, by critics at the end of the nineteenth century. This said, unsurprisingly, during these years a sizable minority of readers always remained who judged Rousseau's political ideas and, more specifically, his "rules for laws" to be ingenious despite their apparent fancifulness. Within this readership during the last century, especially, authors such as Charles Vaughan, Robert Derathé and Ernst Cassirer have emphasized the rationalist features of Rousseau's political system in a way that prioritizes or elevates the status of law.[5] According to Cassirer, for example, the law serves in a very real sense as the "constituent principle" of Rousseau's legitimate state because it alone "confirms

---

[3] Jean Guéhenno, *Jean-Jacques Rousseau*, vol. II (1758–1778), ed. and trans. J. and D. Weightman, New York: Columbia University Press, 1966, 262.

[4] Edmund Burke, *Burke's Politics*, ed. R.S. Hoffman and Paul Levack, New York: Knopf, 1949, 389. Constant writes that Rousseau was "horrorstruck at the immense social power" he had created and "he did not know into whose hands to commit such monstrous force, and he could find no other protection against the danger inseparable from such sovereignty, than an expedient which made its exercise impossible." Benjamin Constant, *Political Writings*, trans. and ed. Biancamaria Fontana, Cambridge and London: Cambridge University Press, 1988, 178. For a more recent view of Rousseau's utopianism see Shklar, *Men and Citizens*, 14–15.

[5] C.E. Vaughan, *The Political Writings of Jean-Jacques Rousseau*, vol. I and II, Cambridge: Cambridge University Press, 1915; Alfred Cobban, *Rousseau and the Modern State*, London: Allen and Unwin, 1934; Robert Derathé, *Le Rationalisme de J.J. Rousseau*, Paris: 1948; Ernst Cassirer, *The Question of Jean-Jacques Rousseau*, trans. P. Gay, New York and New Haven: Yale University Press, 1963 [1954].

and justifies" its existence "spiritually" by making it possible for citizens to be free politically.[6]

Similarly, later authors, such as John B. Noone Jr., Richard Fralin and Jeremy Waldron, call attention to the salience of law in Rousseau's political philosophy while noting the problematic nature of majority decisionmaking generally.[7] Waldron writes, for example, that "the clear consensus in the canon of legal and political thought" is "that the size of a legislative body is an obstacle, rather than an advantage, to rational decisionmaking" and, as such, this process results in "jurisprudential unease about legislation." Originating "in ancient prejudice that surfaced during the Enlightenment," according to Waldron, the source of this unease is that "legislation is not just deliberate, administrative, or political: it is, above all, in the modern world, the product of an *assembly* – the many, the multitude, the rabble (or their representatives)."[8] Large assemblies are perceived to be irrational and inherently demagogic because they are endowed with traits more characteristic of a rabble than of a selectively chosen self-legislating elite. By Giovanni Sartori's account this inability by the people to legislate in any coherent fashion is reinforced by suggestions and recommendations that are intended to ensure that Rousseau's sovereign assembly remains passively docile or "immobile."[9]

How much or how little "jurisprudential unease" is appropriate during lawmaking in Rousseau's state can be argued to be germane to any proper understanding of the political theory of the *Social Contract* and, more broadly, the larger tradition of democratic theory. Investigating this question of lawmaking by large majorities, specifically, this book examines how many of the most well-known

---

[6] Cassirer, *The Question of Jean-Jacques Rousseau*, 63.
[7] John B. Noone, *Rousseau's Social Contract*, Athens, GA: University of Georgia Press, 1980, 36–47; Richard Fralin, *Rousseau and Representation: a Study of the Development of his Concept of Political Institutions*, New York: Columbia University Press, 1978, 54; Jeremy Waldron, *The Dignity of Legislation*, Cambridge: Cambridge University Press, 1999, 31–32.
[8] Waldron, *The Dignity of Legislation*, 31–32.
[9] Giovanni Sartori, *The Theory of Democracy Revisited*, Part II, Chatham: Chatham House, 1987, 314.

republican features in Rousseau's political system are designed to augment, rather than to inhibit, the activity of those persons who are responsible for ratifying the laws. Although, it is indeed true that the Genevan believes that inside of a well-governed polity the laws ought to be relatively stable, it is also his belief that its process ought to be robust with final say over lawmaking residing with the people.

For the philosopher, popular sovereignty can be said to be less about the origin or locus of political authority than its dynamic exercise during legislation. In the *Social Contract*, Rousseau stresses that "it is not through the laws that the State subsists" but "through the legislative power" and that "the law of public order in assemblies is not so much to maintain the general will" as "it is to be sure that it is always questioned and that it always answers" (*CS*, III:xi, 188/424; IV:I, 199/438). Of this relationship, liberty requires that a citizenry be "always questioned" because its authority is less something to be maintained than something to be revealed continuously. Examining the rudiments of the mechanics behind this process, this book explores how what is "always questioned" is made to "always answer" in a way that is both compatible and complementary with republican government. Among other things, I investigate in this book the strengths and weaknesses associated with each of the discrete stages of drafting, ratifying and executing the laws in a bid to refute a burgeoning tradition of distinguished scholars who consider the political role of the people to be marginal. This influential group, which includes Judith N. Shklar, Richard Fralin and Arthur M. Melzer, among others, emphasizes the surreptitious de facto and *de jure* power of elites over the citizenry as the latter is reduced to expressing acclamation for a predetermined legislative agenda. As Steven Johnston remarks, "if Rousseau's texts are read carefully" one finds that "the prominence of law and politics recede" as citizens in his state are reduced to a mere "contrivance of power," an "artifice to be constructed more than an essence to be realized."[10]

---

[10] Steven Johnston, *Encountering Tragedy: Rousseau and the Project of Democratic Order*, Ithaca: Cornell University Press, 1999, 87, 118.

Challenging this dominant viewpoint, I argue in this book that the Genevan goes to great lengths in virtually every avenue of his political system to preserve and, critically, expand the political power of the people. I reveal Rousseau to be a hard-headed political scientist who carefully decompresses the complexities of republican institutions and constitutional government in an effort to enhance, rather than to debilitate, democratic liberty. Consistent with this goal, I illuminate the pragmatics behind the actualization and articulation of his political maxims above his more well-known abstract principles of political right or "universal justice." Focusing less on the audibility of the celestial voice of *la volonté générale* than its legal or political expression, my emphasis is on the institutional aspects of voting above will-formation.

Unlike the voluminous secondary literature on Rousseau's political theory, this book is predominantly about contemporary questions and problems of political science that were anticipated by Rousseau and, to a degree, spoken to by his political philosophy. In this study, each chapter explores a different element of his ideas about lawmaking, and statecraft more generally, that readers describe as opaque. Every chapter investigates a separate stage of his wider legislative process that readers consider obscure or confusing in the context of broader questions of democratic theory.

As all are aware, the relationship between lawmaking and statecraft is less transparent than appears from the Genevan's parsimonious remarks on the subject at the end of Book II of the *Social Contract*. In Book II:xi, he writes that "laws are, properly speaking, only the conditions of the civil association"[11] and "political laws, which constitute the form of Government, are the only ones relevant to my subject."[12] On the surface this statement about legislation as *constitutional* law, expressly, appears uncomplicated so long as what is conveyed by the term, "law," is construed as political law

---

[11] *Social Contract*, II:vi, 154/380.
[12] *Social Contract*, II:xii, 165/394.

exclusively. But for many readers this definition is considered to be overly rigid or narrow because it is possible for a citizenry to vote on constitutional legislation and, as Rousseau comments elsewhere, any civil and criminal laws that can be applied generally. Similar to the political laws, this second and more sweeping domain can be argued to be salient to the extent that it hints at a far more active role for the people in statecraft and civil and criminal lawmaking than is apparent.

Exploring Rousseau's concept of law in Chapter 1, the following chapter examines the issue of legislative initiative (or agenda-setting) and the role of representatives as the drafters of the laws in his mature state. In this section I argue that the theory of the *Social Contract* does not permit interference by representatives in any strong sense during the drafting of the laws but, rather, only afterward or during their execution. Significantly, I explore how Rousseau employs a series of subtle yet practical mechanisms to ensure that those who are responsible for ratifying the laws are never left at the behest of those who initiate them. Deconstructing these mechanisms' workings, I explain why the politically educative and self-reinforcing benefits of democratic participation need not be undermined by the presence of legislative experts during lawmaking and, critically, how such experts can serve a vital function within a "strong democracy" if checked appropriately.

Correspondingly, I investigate in Chapter 3 the most controversial and politically germane of stages in Rousseau's lawmaking process, voting or the ratifying of the laws. Explaining why voting in Rousseau's assembly should not be considered a predetermined act even when the lawgiver indeed proves to be successful at substituting a "partial and moral existence" for man's "physical and independent existence," I illustrate how such interference remains both organically and procedurally constrained in meaningful ways. Of these constraints, I examine in Chapter 4 how Rousseau demonstrates the chief danger to liberty to be not either lawgiving or what James Madison describes in *Federalist* No. 55 as assemblies of "whatever characters composed" but, rather, assemblies of *poorly* composed character. Madison remarks famously that for "all very numerous assemblies, of whatever characters composed, passion never fails to wrest the scepter from reason. Had every Athenian citizen been a Socrates; every Athenian assembly would still have been a mob."[13] With other debilitating vices, the size of an assembly, according to Madison, is what proves to be especially deleterious to popular rule by engendering disorder. Taking this argument at face value, this chapter examines why Rousseau still endorses popular decisionmaking by a large assembly despite the associated political dangers. Noting the many historical authors who associate deliberation in large legislatures with mob rule, I illuminate how Rousseau's political theory is unique in its efforts to evince the possibility of large numbers of people participating in lawmaking without their degenerating into a rabble.

Returning to the topic of Rousseau's utopianism, I explain why the prescribed strictures in the Genevan's constitutional plans for Poland and Corsica are less fancifully impractical than may appear. In Chapter 5, I argue that all of the strictures proposed in these later plans are intended to be examples of realizable political reform but, importantly, only within the constellation of Rousseau's wider social theory. I illustrate how the prescriptions for Poland and Corsica are grounded in a systematically consistent view of human nature that, despite its originality, is not entirely unpersuasive. I spotlight how each of these prescriptions reveals the author's desire for practicality and his willingness to satisfy this impulse by way of a systematic methodology that arises out of a distinct social psychology in which, among other things, sensual or emotional stimuli affect human behavior decisively.

In the last chapter, I take up one of the most understudied or underexplored topics of all within the long history of debate on Rousseau's political thought: adjudication or the *judging* of the laws

---

[13] James Madison, Alexander Hamilton and John Jay, *The Federalist*, Philadelphia: The Franklin Library 1977 [1788], No. 58, 424–425.

in the *Social Contract.* Of this activity, according to a number of interpreters, judging is said not to exist in any substantive sense because all types of legislative interference in sovereign decision-making inevitably divide and usurp the unity of the general will. This said, Maurizio Viroli asserts that among other important institutional checks, "courts represent the specifically constitutional means whereby political order is to be preserved."[14] Earlier, Alfred Cobban is even more certain that "there is to be a separate class of judges" chosen "for their general merit from the whole body of citizens, rather than the modern practice of recruiting them exclusively among the class of legal experts."[15] In this last chapter, I argue that Rousseau does not permit judicial mediation of any sovereign law but he does believe that civil and criminal *decrees* ought to be interpreted by courts. A lesser form of law to be issued or enacted by the government, decrees demand that courts, among other things, scrutinize their applicability to particular or individual cases.

Also in this chapter, I discuss what happens when the laws fail. In a justly-ordered state any temporary suspension of the sovereign power can be shown to result from a myriad of different causes without any one necessarily leading to its ultimate demise. When the laws must be suspended and how a citizenry is to regain legislative control is an important question in view of the actual history of constitutional dictatorship in republican Rome. One obvious answer to this question is that if a polity were truly well-ordered then any dictator that would arise would follow the example of republican-minded Cincinnatus and place love of *patrie* first and voluntarily depart. But this may be an overly idealistic assumption. Controversially, Rousseau believes that the greatest danger is the people's reluctance to choose a dictator when necessary. Examining the logic behind his argument for dictatorship in Chapter IV:vi of the *Social Contract* within the context of the later history of republican Rome, I argue

---

[14] Maurizio Viroli, *Jean Jacques Rousseau and the Well-Ordered Society,* trans. Derek Hanson, Cambridge: Cambridge University Press, 1988, 214.

[15] Cobban, *Rousseau and the Modern State,* 81–82.

that any temporary suspension of the laws in Rousseau's state should not be regarded as posing as lethal a threat to liberty as some may construe to be the case. I examine and weigh the Genevan's rationale for choosing a dictator over other alternatives and the merits of this choice relative to other options during a military or constitutional emergency.

Taken together, each of these chapters seeks to highlight Rousseau's bearing as a legislator and political craftsman. As a contribution to the wider body of literature on the *Social Contract*, I reveal how his thoughts on lawmaking are not anchored solely to his detailed and lengthy ruminations on the merits of the wise and illustrious lawgivers of old. The activity of realizing the general will in the *Social Contract* can be viewed holistically in the sense of encompassing disparate aspects of a remarkably systematic legislative process. Surprisingly, some of the most unusually original elements of this process emerge only after the laws are drafted and the lawgiver departs from the scene. What happens to the laws procedurally at every stage of lawmaking is fundamental to understanding how liberty is given concrete expression in the institutions of the *Social Contract*. More pointedly, what happens across each of these stages illustrates Rousseau's astuteness or even brilliance as a constitutionalist in a way that burnishes his reputation as one of the greatest political minds of the modern world.

1   Rousseau's concept of law

Liberty in the *Social Contract* is achieved not by the stability or continuity of the laws but by what Jean Starobinski describes as the political contextualization of *la transparence*: the ability or inability of a community to free itself from the arbitrary preferences of its members politically.[1] In a legitimate state it is the possibility of this transparency, specifically, that gives substance to liberty to the extent that what individuals prefer is not guided by any capricious wants or desires but by the rationalized will of the community as a whole. Each prefers the good of all without preferring the good of each during the consideration of his or her own private interests. Fundamentally different from other expressions of dependency in society, it is by way of the reciprocity and coercive nature of the laws, according to Rousseau, that this relationship is universalized and elevated into something other than an alternative form of *l'obstacle*. It is owing to the laws that liberty is no longer arbitrary but grounded in justice.

Asking "what is a law after all?" in reply to this question the philosopher emphasizes the generality of the popular vote as a means to achieving *la transparence*. When "an entire people enacts something concerning the entire people, it considers only itself" and "the subject matter of the enactment is general like the will that enacts. It is this act that I call a law" (*CS*, II:vi, 153/379). Expressly,

---

[1] "The *Social Contract* postulates a simultaneous alienation of wills, in which each person ultimately receives back from the collectivity whatever he voluntarily cedes to it." By both willing the law and obeying it as a unity, "each man sees and loves himself in others, for the greater unity of all." Jean Starobinski, *Jean-Jacques Rousseau: Transparency and Obstruction*, trans. Arthur Goldhammer, intro. Robert J. Morrissey, Chicago and London: The University of Chicago Press, 1988 [1971], 97.

> the matter and form of the Laws constitute their nature. The
> form consists of the authority that enacts laws; the matter
> consists of the thing enacted ... As the thing enacted is
> necessarily related to the common good, it follows that the
> object of the law should be general, as is the will dictating it; and
> it is this double universality which creates the true character of
> the Law.
>
> *(MG, II:iv, 111/327)*

Of this close identification between "the thing enacted" and
the common good it is by way of the activity of legislating the laws
that reason serves to correct and universalize the atomistic interests
of community members in a way that permits the collectivity to
"consider only itself." This close identification, in part the product
of a successful social engineering that harmonizes individual preferences and the common good, is reinforced by the reciprocity of
the laws. Even more than external interference, during meetings of
the assembly it is the reciprocity of the laws that serves to level the
angularity of human sentiment by generalizing each citizen's consideration of his or her particular interests. According to Rousseau,
"if law cannot be unjust, it is not because justice is its basis, which
might not always be true, but because it is contrary to nature for one
to want to harm himself, which is true without exception" (*MG*,
II:iv, 113/329). When each votes for himself by voting for all it is this
truth "without exception" that ensures that the private interest of
every individual is in conformity with the good of the community.
When this happens, by "substituting justice for instinct" and replacing "physical impulse" and "appetite" with the "voice of duty," each
person will "consult his reason before heeding his inclinations."
And this is critical. Although a source of social, psychological and
political dependency in a different context, reason is a source of both
liberty and justice when the reciprocity of the laws compels each
individual to identify solely with the common good of the whole.

Significantly, it is vital to stress that by "generality" what
Rousseau means is actually "universality" and, as he notes in the

Social Contract, each of these two terms are interchangeable (*CS,* II:iv, 111–112/327).[2] This universality is such that each must experience the laws' obligations with equal force. For "every authentic act of the general will obligates or favors all Citizens equally" and true equity is assured only when everyone votes for laws knowing that their effect won't place him at a disadvantage relative to his neighbor (*CS,* II:iv, 149/374).[3] Highlighting this point, he emphasizes that it is actual burdens, rather than merely formal obligations, that are primary and that the assembly cannot "burden one subject more than another" or even ask "another to do what he himself does not do" (*CS,* II:iv, 150/375; III:xvi, 194/432). It is the laws' strict impersonality or universality, beyond their logical generality, that produces "an equality between the citizens such that they all engage themselves under the same conditions and should all benefit from the same rights." In the end, "the force of legislation should always tend to maintain" a perfect equality (*CS,* II:iv, 149/374; II:xi, 163/392).

---

[2] This view is argued for convincingly by Noone. "Mere logical generality" is insufficient for achieving equity and inequality can occur unless the laws' force is experienced by all equally. The possibility of such an outcome would destroy sovereign unity by giving those persons who may be affected adversely grounds not to vote. Arthur M. Melzer writes that "only through general laws that apply equally to each" is justice attainable but, as Noone explains, such a logical generality by itself does not assure that the laws will "apply equally to each." The one exception to this rule would be a law that regulates a scarce privilege in which "the criteria of distribution" would have to be such that no citizen is debarred from acquiring it. Possession of the privilege must not be inequitable enough to achieve "personal authority over others." See John B. Noone, *Rousseau's Social Contract,* Athens, GA: University of Georgia Press, 1980, 37–40; Arthur M. Melzer, *The Natural Goodness of Man: On The System of Rousseau's Thought,* Chicago: The University of Chicago Press, 1990, 153.

[3] Vaughan appears to admit the laws formal equity only. He sees the generality of taxation laws, for example, as "a plain instance of discrimination between class and class, between one section of the community and another." In my view, this reading places too much emphasis on the narrowly formal aspects of a law because it is equity of outcome that is most essential to Rousseau. During any vote, such as one on a proposed tax law, the initiative to be decided must avoid any inequitable outcome if unanimity or even a majority is to be possible. Of this principle of equity, I agree with Noone's view that "a tax that applies exclusively or differentially to one sector of society is, on the face of it, discriminatory and thus not a law." C.E. Vaughan, *The Political Writings of Jean-Jacques Rousseau,* vol. I, Cambridge: Cambridge University Press, 1915, 67. Noone, *Rousseau's Social Contract,* 42.

In Rousseau's political system, such a perfect equality will never be at odds with liberty because the latter is different from the traditional view of freedom, or Berlinian "negative liberty."[4] In an often cited passage from his *Letters Written from the Mountain*, Rousseau famously describes justice as turning on the distinction between *l'indépendence* and *la liberté*, writing that "liberty consists less in doing one's will than in not being subject to someone else's" (*LEM*, VIII, 260–261/841–842). This "not being subject" to another's will is true liberty in the broadest sense of the term because it takes into account the impact of others on the formation of one's preferences that, almost always, individuals misconstrue as freedom. Such *l'independence* or liberty through the laws is a kind of freedom in which men are psychologically, materially and politically autonomous from each other's wills in a circular fashion. Such autonomy is realized in a circular fashion: no vote counts more than any other; no burden counts more than any other and the only form of dependency experienced is by the individual vis-à-vis the group. Rousseau believes that whenever an individual "submits himself to the conditions he imposes on others" he is truly autonomous because he votes only his own preferences and interests and he is also truly just because he ensures that all receive the same rights and benefits that he wishes for himself. Although each person's vote reflects only his "preference for himself" it is in accordance with the common good because every voter construes his or her own private preferences in the same way ideally (*CS*, II:iv, 149/373–374).

Rejecting negative freedom, Rousseau repudiates any Hobbesian "silence of the laws"[5] as self-defeating because each person will *inevitably* submit to his or her neighbor's will unless a solution, political

---

4 "Political liberty in this sense is simply the area within which a man can act unobstructed by others. If I am prevented by others from doing what I could otherwise do, I am to that degree unfree ... You lack political liberty or freedom only if you are prevented from attaining a goal by human beings." Isaiah Berlin, *Four Essays on Liberty*, Oxford and New York: Oxford University Press, 1969, 122.

5 *Leviathan*, XXI:xviii.

or otherwise, is found. Beneath such a "silence" individuals' private and public judgments will be mediated by the perceptions of others to a degree that *l'independence* or autonomy is obstructed. Because "prejudices themselves have their progression and rules" it is "these rules to which the public is subject without suspecting" (*RJJ*, III, 236/964–965) when guided by those persons who endeavor to give them direction surreptitiously. Ultimately, all citizens will behave as others do, adopt the values of the group, covet appearance and chase distinction as popular norms, replace or supplant independent thinking and decisionmaking. In this condition a "silence of the laws" connotes nothing other than tacit conformity or, worse, obsequiousness before the self-appointed arbiters of opinion who set the rules that direct men's prejudices.

Critically, in the *Social Contract* Rousseau explains that even within the best *patrie* lawmaking is never entirely transparent to the extent that any law is guided by reason solely. Contrary to Immanuel Kant's view in the *Metaphysics of Morals*, lawmaking can never be endowed with the certitude of a mathematical formula or a logical proof, according to Rousseau.[6] So long as individuals live together in society then desire, emotion, sentiment, superstition, prejudice and, most egregiously, *amour-propre* must inevitably color each person's understanding of his or her own particular interests. He asks "where is the man who can be so objective about himself?" answering that "no one will deny that the general will in each individual is a pure act of understanding, which reasons in the silence of the passions" that sometimes fail to keep quiet (*MG*, I:ii, 80/286).

The complexity of the dichotomous relationship between reason and passion can be appreciated by Joshua Cohen's restating of the foundational question at the origin of Rousseau's compact: "What kind of association would be rationally agreed to by socially interdependent individuals who are moved by self-love and, above all, by

---

[6] See Alexander Kaufman, "Reason, Self-Legislation and Legitimacy: Conceptions of Freedom in the Political Thought of Rousseau and Kant," *Review of Politics*, 59 (1) 1997: 25–52.

an interest in securing their freedom?"[7] Reason, self-love and interest each play a role in securing freedom and yet none can be easily
reconciled in even the most well-ordered of states.

Rousseau's lack of an easily digestible solution to this tension
has led some readers to conclude that in his political writings he
is "genuinely unable to make up his mind about what constitutes
the general will and how it comes to be,"[8] but, arguably, this is not
the case. Rather, it can be asserted that it is the unfamiliarity and
originality of the *Social Contract*'s solution to the problem of achieving *la transparence* that is confusing and not the solution itself. Of
this unfamiliarity, it is the combination of passion and reason that
reveals why perfect unanimity during the vote is rare and why there
is no such thing as a Rousseauian "ideal state" in the sense of a political community in which citizens give a perfect corporeal expression
to the general will with any regularity. Unlike Plato's philosopher-
king who shares in the Forms, Rousseau's sovereign-members are
hobbled by the vagaries or uncertainties that accompany human passion but this does not mean, as Joseph Schumpeter would later comment influentially, that there can never be such a thing as a "general
will."[9] Roger D. Masters explains that it is owing to human passion

---

[7] Cohen writes, "Rousseau's argument that the general will is the solution to the
   social contract" has "two main elements, corresponding to the considerations
   of self-love and freedom that figure in the description of the contract. The fact
   that the social order ought to advance common interests corresponds to the fact
   that the contract is a unanimous agreement among rational individuals who are
   moved by self-love." See Joshua Cohen, "Reflections on Rousseau: Autonomy and
   Democracy," in Christopher Morris, ed., *The Social Contract Theorists*, Lanham
   and New York: Rowman and Littlefield, 1999, 192, 193.

[8] Richard Fralin, *Rousseau and Representation: a Study of the Development of his
   Concept of Political Institutions*, New York: Columbia University Press, 1978,
   86–87. Vaughan remarks that the Genevan "may not always be consistent in
   working out this conception." Ripstein attributes this ambiguity less to confusion by Rousseau than to a simple lack of clarity, that "Rousseau never explicitly
   defines the general will, and the task of making sense of it is made harder still
   by the fact that he does not provide a clear account of what he takes individual
   willing to be." See Vaughan, *The Political Writings of Jean-Jacques Rousseau*, I,
   28; Arthur Ripstein, "The General Will," in Christopher Morris, ed., *The Social
   Contract Theorists*, Lanham and New York: Rowman and Littlefield, 1999, 220.

[9] Joseph A. Schumpeter, *Capitalism, Socialism and Democracy*, London: Allen
   and Unwin, 1943, 250–268.

that an inherent tension is manifest between subjects' self-interests and the common good that serves to impede any smooth or "friction-less" lawmaking.[10] It is because of this tension that the interests of representatives or magistrates can never be wholly identical to that of the people and, significantly, why the sovereign-body experiences obstacles at achieving unanimity while voting. Rousseau's belief is that even if the social bond "were as well established as possible" all "difficulties would not disappear." For "the works of men – always less perfect than those of nature – never go so directly toward their end ... the general will is rarely the will of all, and the public force is always less than the sum of private forces" (*MG*, I:iv, 88/296–297).

Contrary to Masters' reading, however, I believe that it can be shown that Rousseau considers unanimity to be achievable despite its rarity.[11] Instances of unanimity during voting may be infrequent but such instances will occur and the Genevan believes that among sovereign-members perfect agreement is possible before and after the end of the transitional epoch of the state's founding (bookmarked by the arrival and departure of the lawgiver). His belief is that so long as the "social tie" has not entirely slackened or unraveled then the need to create new laws will indeed be "universally seen." When this transpires then "several men together consider themselves to be a single body" and, like peasants beneath an oak tree, transparency is such that "all of the mechanisms of the State are vigorous and simple ...

---

[10] See Roger D. Masters, *The Political Philosophy of Rousseau*, Princeton: Princeton University Press, 1968, 285–286, 301–305.

[11] In my opinion, Masters' explanation of the inherent "tension" between human self-interestedness and collective decisionmaking is accurate but its effects are overstated. I concur with Melzer that Rousseau, in part, considers the general will to be "an outgrowth of self-interest" and that it is possible for persons to have "a permanent selfish interest in the common good" (*The Natural Goodness of Man*, 164). Although the Genevan's mechanical metaphor appears to illustrate the impossibility of achieving unanimity, Rousseau himself uses the word "rare" instead of "impossible" in the express passages where the question is considered. The other terms that Rousseau employs are "clearly appar-ent," "vigorous and simple," "clear and luminous," "no tangled, contradictory interests" and "universally seen" when describing a process that is supposedly impossible to achieve fully (*CS*, IV:i, 198/437).

it has no tangled, contradictory interests, the common good is clearly apparent everywhere, and requires only good sense to be perceived" (*CS*, IV:i, 198/437).

This said, it is owing to the tension between human passion and self-interestedness and collective decisionmaking that Rousseau refrains from proposing any idealized type of political structure.[12] He articulates formal standards of political legitimacy with respect to sovereignty but he does not impose any rigid or specific governmental type to execute the decisions rendered in accordance with these standards. Exhibiting a preference for elective aristocratic government because of its better aligning of magisterial and popular interests ("the best of Governments is the aristocratic; the worst of Sovereignties is the aristocratic," *LEM*, VI, 233/808–809), this and all other regime-types fall under his practical or prudential "maxims of politics" rather than beneath the more formal or abstract "principles of political right" that inform how laws are to be legislated in order to be considered obligatory.

Of this lack of rigidity with respect to regime-type, where the term can be said to be appropriate, what Rousseau considers to be "ideal" is whatever comes closest to satisfying the conditions by which transparency is realizable during the laws' enactment. Among other things, these conditions are affected by external and diverse variables such as climate, geography and economics or less tangible forces that help to influence the character of a people. Irrespective of their government, Rousseau labels any state in which the people are both the source and the object of the Laws as being "republican:" "Every State ruled by Laws" is "a Republic" and "whatever the form of administration ... every legitimate Government is republican" (*CS*, II:vi, 153/379–380) so long as the people are the ultimate legislative authority.

---

[12] "when one asks which is absolutely the best Government, one poses a question that is insoluble because it is indeterminate. Or, if you prefer, it has as many correct answers as there are possible combinations in the absolute and relative situations of people" (*CS*, III:ix, 185/419).

Significantly, Rousseau considers the tension between passion and reason during lawmaking to be resolvable to the extent that the latter acts to universalize the particularity of the former to make the laws moral. For the "impulse of appetite *alone* is slavery, and obedience to the law one has prescribed for oneself is freedom" (*CS*, I:viii, 141–142/364–365; my italics).[13] Reason does not supplant or replace passion but, rather, as Alexander Kaufman comments, it serves as its corrective.[14] Similar to Alexis de Tocqueville who believes that the "inner voice" of passion is "formed only by the habit of judging and feeling within society and according to its laws" in *Democracy in America*, Rousseau emphasizes the importance of reason to the proper interpretation of this inner voice's dictates. What matters most to the actualizing of liberty is the "habit of judging and feeling" in combination, according to Rousseau, just as Tocqueville believes that "the habits that have sprung from freedom" are more significant than the mere "love of freedom itself."[15]

Of these habits of judging and feeling, Rousseau believes that the role of the lawgiver is to guide the mores, customs and traditions of a people in a way that fosters obedience to law while, critically, making sure that the latter themselves correspond to their psychological and situational disposition. The lawgiver's "science"

---

[13] Relative to the moral liberty that exists in a well-governed state, persons in the state of nature experience only a *kind* of slavery. Rousseau believes that individuals in the state of nature are "free agents" to the extent that each is able to deviate from instinct "often to his detriment" (*DI*, I, 26/141). Against Plato and the ancient mindset, Rousseau believes that what distinguishes humans from animals is not reason, but freedom, although such a weak expression of freedom in the form of path-independence from instinct is slight or meager relative to moral liberty.

[14] Kaufman, "Reason, Self-Legislation and Legitimacy," 25–52. This is not to be confused with Rousseau's belief that the general will is incapable of being made "right" by the bulk of the citizenry. "It is never a question of correcting it," according to the Genevan, "but it is necessary to know how to consult it appropriately" (*MG*, I:vii, 99/311). Similar to Plato's view of knowledge the general will is made explicit by way of a process of discovery and Rousseau's fear is that during this endeavor citizens may be led astray inadvertently by their "love of the beautiful." This peril is what necessitates resort to a lawgiver.

[15] Alexis de Tocqueville, *Democracy in America*, ed. J.P. Mayer, trans. George Lawrence, New York: Harper and Row, 1969, 243.

is to read the situation on the ground, so to speak, and to know how to draft legislative initiatives that are closely matched to a people's character, temperament and external environment (CS, II:vi, 152/378; MG, II:ii, 102–103/314–315; LA, 61/299). More likely to garner success than efforts at "transforming human nature," Rousseau repeatedly stresses the need for the lawgiver to adapt the laws to the people, rather than vice versa, because there is little help to be given to a people who have already lived beneath past laws. He believes that a corrupted people cannot be purified and an uncorrupted people need only to be emotionally "refashioned" in the sense of a greater or deeper corporate unity. Importantly, those most fortunate of peoples who are truly ripe for lawgiving because they have not yet known the yoke of any other law or have had their memories wiped away by cataclysmic events are extraordinarily rare (CS, II:x, 162/391; MG, II:iii, 105, 109–110/319, 324–325) owing to "the impossibility of finding the simplicity of nature together with the needs of society. All of these conditions, it is true, are hard to find together. Hence one sees few well-constituted states" (CS, II:x, 162/391).[16]

NATURAL LAW

In Rousseau's political writings the laws serve as the divine basis of legal and political obligation. In a legitimate state, political justice is the corporeal expression of God's "heavenly" or "celestial voice" as it

---

[16] The conditions that must be in place for a people to be receptive to the lawgiver's tutelage are exceedingly great even by Rousseau's estimate. He asks, "What people, then, is suited for legislation? One that, though already bound by some union of origin, interest or convention, has not yet borne the true yoke of laws. One that has neither customs nor superstitions that are deeply entrenched. One that does not fear being crushed by a sudden invasion and can, without becoming involved in its neighbors' quarrels, resist each of them by itself or use the help of one to drive away another. One where each member can be known to all, and where it is not necessary to impose on any man a greater burden than a man can bear. One that does not depend on other peoples, and on whom no other people depends. One that is neither rich nor poor, and can be self-sufficient. Finally, one that combines the stability of an ancient people with the docility of a new people" (CS, II:x, 162/390–391).

is elevated into a religious precept. Rousseau's belief is that because natural law is unknowable in the state of nature and both incomprehensible and unenforceable in modern society, the only possible basis for political obligation is agreement.[17] The "social order is a sacred right" that is "founded on conventions" which provide the only intelligible norm for political obligation and justice. He asserts that "all justice comes from God" but "if we knew how to receive it from on high, we would need neither government nor laws" (CS, II:iii, 152/378).

In this regard, prior to the social pact it is impossible to define justice because human cognition is simply too underdeveloped. For the "concepts of the natural law" begin to "develop only when the prior development of the passions renders all of its precepts impotent" and any societally imposed conditions of community are such that "men must necessarily be in ignorance of them or violate them" (MG, I:ii, 78/284). Their tenets are unclear because they are "drawn from several kinds of Knowledge which men do not naturally have, and from advantages of which men can only conceive the idea after having left the State of Nature" (DI, preface, 14/125).

Considering this void, the most that individuals can ascertain with respect to such tenets is a set of highly generalized precepts that are too unspecific to be binding in any legal sense. Without any certain knowledge of God's will on earth it is left to individuals to utilize reason to "reestablish upon other foundations" (DI, preface, 14–15/125–126) all of the rules of right essential to human relations and, more narrowly, legitimate government. Unlike the erroneous "other foundations" that serve as the basis of law in modern society after reason "has succeeded in stifling Nature," in a truly well-governed state this substructure must always be the product of

---

[17] The tenets of natural law are unknown because "the development of society stifles humanity in men's hearts by awakening personal interest, and that concepts of the natural law, which should rather be called the law of reason, begin to develop only when the prior development of the passions renders all of its precepts impotent" (MG, I:ii, 78/284).

agreement and consensus. Because men are not naturally sociable creatures justice must be entirely self-created.[18]

Similar to Hugo Grotius, Samuel Pufendorf and other modern natural rights theorists, Rousseau does not believe that obedience to natural law is ever voluntary. Natural law will never be commonly or routinely obeyed by individuals, as Diderot wrongly asserts,[19] because without the threat of the sword men's passions are thwarting. In the absence of a sufficient enforcement mechanism those persons who would voluntarily obey natural law render themselves vulnerable to those who would not and, owing to this contradiction, the law cannot be logically binding. Collectively, few individuals would agree to a compact where reciprocity toward anything is never assured; most would opt for self-protection above the shield of a feckless prince. To remedy this problem there must be "guarantees against all unjust undertakings" (*MG*, I:ii, 79/285) as the likelihood that others might evade prosecution gives *everyone* justification to evade punishment or to rely on oneself for safety.[20]

Rejecting parental authority, coercion or voluntary submission to a conqueror as a basis for obligation, as a solution Rousseau believes that the mutual goals of security and liberty are realized elsewhere. As Ernst Cassirer describes, "Law in its pure and strict sense is not a mere external bond that holds in individuals' wills and prevents their scattering; rather it is the constituent principle of

---

[18] Melzer writes that justice cannot be discerned naturally and "the state is needed to teach justice as well as enforce it." Justice "is not something natural, but wholly a creature of the artificial state" because it alone can ensure reciprocity with respect to law. Arthur M. Melzer, "Rousseau's Moral Realism: Replacing Natural Law with the General Will," *American Political Science Review*, 77, June 1983, 638–640.

[19] Denis Diderot, "Natural Right," from the *Encyclopedia* (vol. V) in C.E. Vaughan, *The Political Writings of Jean-Jacques Rousseau*, I, 431.

[20] Rousseau asserts that "the advantages of the social law would be fine if while I were scrupulously observing it toward others, I were sure that all of them would observe it toward me. But what assurance of this can you give me, and could there be a worse situation for me than to be exposed to all the ills that stronger men would want to cause me without my daring to make up for it against the weak?" (*MG*, I:ii, 79/285).

these wills."[21] This principle, the general will made concrete, solves the "fundamental problem" of the social compact by revealing how it is possible to both "defend and protect the person and goods of each associate" and remain "as free as before" (CS, I:vi, 138/360). How citizens are able to express their political freedom in a way that is simultaneously non-discriminatory (security) and autonomous (liberty) is by living under a set of general laws that affect everybody in a reciprocal way.

Fundamental law

Unlike Hobbes who dimly concludes that he "could never see in any author what a fundamental law signifieth" (Leviathan, II:xxvi, 42), Rousseau signifies it very specifically as the common good expressed by the general will. What is and is not "fundamental" is decided by the vote alone although the outcome of this decision ought never to be contrary to the vague precepts of natural law if the sovereign laws are to be legitimate. Fundamental law ought always to be wholly uncontroversial as "all the mechanisms of the State are vigorous and simple" and its maxims "clear and luminous." For "the institution of laws is not such a marvelous thing that any man of sense and equity could not easily find those which, well observed, would be the most beneficial for society" (LA, 299/61). Such laws can be said to be fundamental in the sense that each is constitutive of institutions that are the best of all possibilities for realizing the common good.

As Melissa Schwartzberg describes, the static and binding nature of the fundamental laws together with Rousseau's seemingly contradictory demand for a "free vote of the people" are reconcilable.[22] This original tension appears in Poland, for example, in the

---

[21] Ernst Cassirer, The Question of Jean-Jacques Rousseau, trans. P. Gay, New York and New Haven: Yale University Press, 1963 [1954], 63.

[22] Melissa Schwartzberg, "Rousseau on Fundamental Law," Political Studies, 51, 2003, 387–403. In her essay, Schwartzberg adopts Stephen Holmes' "enabling model" to demonstrate how it is possible to reconcile fundamental law with a dynamic general will or a "free vote of the people." Holmes' explanation of the enabling aspects of constitutional self-binding or view that constitutional

Genevan's seemingly contradictory observation that the laws must be "as irrevocable as they can be" despite the fact that "it is against the nature of the body politic to impose on itself laws that it cannot revoke" (*CGP*, 203–204/996). Unlike earlier natural rights theorists, though, he appears to construe fundamental law as being *ex post* rather than *ex ante* to sovereign lawmaking and revocable by way of a single vote (*CS*, III:xviii, 197/436).[23] Addressing this tension, Schwartzberg comments that "it is inappropriate to consider this fundamental law a true restriction on the ability of the sovereign to enact its will; the general will, by definition, is the greatest good of all, and thus public utility is merely a constitutive rule."[24] Freedom and law are compatible because "the free vote of the people" always results in an outcome that is consistent with public utility in a legitimate state. Liberty and the general will are congruent with public utility because the people cannot vote for a law that is contrary to their own common good. Conversely, any divide between law and liberty can be manifest only when the former is in a state of decline. Individuals will mistake their particular interests for the public weal when the political institutions that give substance and force to sovereign lawmaking have eroded.

Similar to Hobbes' view that "for a fundamental law in every commonwealth is that which, being taken away, the commonwealth

restraints are what makes democracy viable, rather than what impedes it, is shown to be useful (though not entirely analogous) to the status of fundamental law in Rousseau's just state.

23 Charles Hendel attributes this unique rendering of fundamental law to Rousseau. Hendel writes that "the superior power must always be kept where it first exists, in the whole body of the people. They are the sovereign and they can never give up anything of their sovereignty without ceasing to be a political body. They impose the obligations to obey the law on themselves, and it is they who really enforce them, not any external authority. The 'fundamental laws,' as they were called, are nothing but the settled expression of their general will. Their power to make new law and to order their own affairs is the fundamental thing and it is never alienated or destroyed unless they cease to exist at all as a community. Thus the doctrine of 'fundamental laws' must be ushered out of court along with that spurious pact which robs the people of their own sovereignty." Charles Hendel, *Jean-Jacques Rousseau: Moralist*, I, Oxford and London: Oxford University Press, 149.

24 Schwartzberg, "Rousseau on Fundamental Law," 392.

faileth and is utterly dissolved, as a building whose foundation is destroyed" (*Leviathan*, II:xxvi, 43), Rousseau believes that no legitimate state can exist in the absence of fundamental law. It is only in a corrupt state that a citizenry would choose institutions that are contrary to fundamental law and such a gross violation is possible only if a people is too ignorant or too venal to recognize the general will. For "various relations have to be considered in order to organize the whole or give the commonwealth the best possible form" and

> the laws that regulate this relationship are named political laws and are also called fundamental laws, not without a degree of reason if these laws are wise. For if there is only one correct way to organize each State, the people that has found it should abide by it; but if the established order is bad, why should one accept as fundamental, laws that prevent it from being good? Besides, in any event a people is always the master to change its laws – even the best laws; for if it wishes to do itself harm, who has the right to prevent it from doing so?
>
> (*CS, II:xii, 104/393–394*)

In this regard, it is only those laws that are "wise" and in harmony with the common good that can be called fundamental and the people ought to be able to change any "bad law" that was once accepted "as fundamental" if it is harmful.

SOVEREIGN LAWS AND EXECUTIVE DECREES

Any civil or criminal act can be considered to be a sovereign law so long as its source and its object is the people. This said, in Book II:xi, Rousseau remarks that "political laws, which constitute the form of Government, are the only ones relevant to my subject" (*CS*, II:xii, 165/394) and it appears that this qualifier is intended to exclude civil and criminal law. Whether or not this is truly the case, though, is unclear because he writes elsewhere that the sovereign can "designate the qualities" that entitle membership to "Classes of Citizens" (*CS*, II:vi, 153/379) so the assembly could, presumably, confer privileges or ratify a tax code so long as the effects of the law are not manifest in a way that is discriminatory or results in a greater political, economic or social inequality. Arguably, the chief source of confusion regarding this qualifier can be said to turn on the somewhat veiled differences between sovereign "Laws" (with a capital "L" in Rousseau's corpus) that are ratified by the citizenry in their collective capacity and, less authoritatively, "decrees" that are enacted by the government. As many are aware, throughout his political writings the word "legislation" refers expressly to the former while "particular laws" refers to the latter or administrative decrees.

For first-time readers of the *Social Contract* the two categories "Laws" and "decrees" may appear to be similar but their differences are germane to any coherent understanding of its author's political theory. Significantly, the most salient distinction between the two types of legal acts is their relative measure of authority: only an act that is ratified by the people as a whole has the authority of a sovereign Law (with a capital "L") and any measure that is issued by the government is subordinate to it; such an ancillary measure cannot be contrary to either the word or spirit of the general will as it is expressed in the Laws.[25]

More narrowly, the laws are a set of generalized formal rules relating to the structure of a legitimate state while executive or

---

[25] Over the course of the lifespan of the state any differences between the two types of legal acts should be marginalized because the lawgiver is responsible for drafting both "Laws" and decrees. Any angularity between the two should be leveled down because administrative decrees would not be a set of discretionary rules imposed by government but, at least in the early years of the state, a set of wholly non-discretionary rules inherited from the same organ that drafts the sovereign laws. This can be seen, for example, when Rousseau describes the lawgiver's efforts to guide customs, *moeurs* and opinion *en secret* by way of "particular regulations" (*CS*, II:xii, 165/394). *En secret*, such particular regulations are drafted by the lawgiver rather than by the government and are revealed to be something other than the initiatives of the prince. In this respect, those who are responsible for enacting decrees are never permitted to do so in a vacuum but, rather, must remain sensitive to the general will. Any inherited powers of the prince *must* be administered in a way that is congruent with its tenets. As I discuss elsewhere, unlike the sovereign laws, any particular law passed by the executive is available to mediation by the courts without such interference resulting in an illegitimate division of sovereignty.

administrative decrees are a set of particularized commands relating to this structure's proper function. Of this proper function, decrees pertain to distinct categories, classes or ranks of persons in a way that could never be assured of achieving unanimity or expediency if put up before a popular vote. Intended to aid the state at operating smoothly, decrees facilitate statecraft in all areas where popular decisionmaking would be wholly illegitimate, ineffective or dangerous. Specific to particular issues of national defense, public order, education, the selective distribution of burdens (such as state taxes, civic duties) or the bestowing of rewards (public honors, magisterial offices, privileges, etc.) decrees give content to the laws as they regulate social, civil and economic relations at the everyday level. Although both categories of legal acts, laws and decrees, impinge upon the life of the citizen as the *moi commun* and *moi particulier* in diverse ways, it is the latter that mostly regulates the microlife of community-members.

According to Rousseau, the relative generality of the two categories of legal acts' ends is of key importance. Every sovereign law has to be general in its object but it is permissible and even expected for a decree to apply to only a part of the population. Although the number of legislators for both types of legal acts will vary within all regimes that are not democracies, this difference is less significant than whether or not every citizen is bound by the laws equally. For example, a regulation that is passed by the entire community can never be considered to be a Law if it is directed toward only a tiny minority of the population or a single person, according to Rousseau. Conversely, a measure that applies to everybody may still be considered to be a Law despite its rejection by a sizable minority of voters. So long as an initiative receives a majority of all of the votes counted it is still a Law but differences in the size of a majority will enhance or diminish its legitimacy.

This said, critically, it must be remembered that only the people as a whole can vote; no magistrate or elected delegate can ever be said to "represent" the people's will beyond the latter's own tacit acceptance of (less authoritative) governmental decrees. All of the people must vote for all of the sovereign laws personally if a state is to be considered legitimate. Logistically difficult to achieve in practice, of course, Rousseau considers this goal to be a realizable ideal.

Among other authors, such as G.D.H. Cole, Bertrand de Jouvenal believes that what is most relevant is the laws' universality or impersonality irrespective of the number of actual voters in Rousseau's state.[26] What is said to matter solely is the generality of the laws' object, regardless of the actual percentage of voters who attend the assembly. By "percentage of voters" I mean the percentage of *eligible* voting citizenry (which is itself a topic of considerable controversy because Rousseau's definition of citizenship appears to exclude women).[27] According to this reading, it is the Genevan's definition of the "common interest" in Book II:iv of the *Social Contract* that is most germane. In this chapter, he writes that "what generalizes the will is not so much the number of votes as the common interest that unites them" (*CS*, II:iv, 149/374), blatantly contradicting his later statement in Book II:vi that the general will is discoverable only "when the entire people enacts something concerning the entire people" (*CS*, II:vi, 153/379).

Challenging this well-known interpretation, it can be argued that if readers carefully scrutinize this question in the revisions to the *Social Contract* against the earlier draft of the *Geneva Manuscript*, it is apparent that Rousseau believes that *all* of the people must vote for a law to be considered legitimate. He was aware that his earlier draft was potentially misleading on the topic of the laws' generality and his

---

[26] Bertrand de Jouvenal, *Sovereignty*, Chicago and London: The University of Chicago Press, 1957, 93.

[27] Although Rousseau is a man of his century I find it noteworthy that he says so little about the political prohibitions against women in the *Social Contract*. It may be possible to make a persuasive counter-argument to the traditional view that women cannot vote in his state. On this question in his political writings, see Joel Schwartz, *The Sexual Politics of Jean-Jacques Rousseau*, Chicago and London: The University of Chicago Press, 1984, 41–47; Lori Jo Marso, *(Un) Manly Citizens: Jean-Jacques Rousseau's and Germaine de Staël's Subversive Women*, Baltimore and London: Johns Hopkins University Press, 1999, 5.

remark that "what generalizes the will is not so much the number of votes as the common interest" refers to the size of a voting majority solely. Not inconsequentially, the revised text clarifies the sentence above to refer to the number of votes (*"le nombre des voix"*) *received* on a legislative initiative, expressly, instead of the number of actual voters (*"la quantité des votans"*) in absolute terms (*CS*, II:vi, 149/374; *MG*, I:vi, 96/307). Notably, the remainder of this passage continues, "because everyone necessarily submits himself to the conditions that he imposes on others," which can only occur when all citizens personally "impose" such conditions by voting. Ideally, all of the citizenry ought to vote on every sovereign law in perfect unanimity but this requirement is not mandatory for a decision to be considered an act of sovereignty. But all of the citizenry must or should participate in lawmaking and every potential voter who fails to do so diminishes the legitimacy of the activity's outcome.

Conversely, decrees that are enacted by just a small percentage of citizens who are authorized to serve in a purely executive capacity may be considered to be an indirect expression of the general will so long as the people as a whole do not thwart them. Such particular measures are devoid of the authority of a sovereign law and they can be thwarted by a citizenry in various indirect ways, such as by passing new laws, changing the form of the executive or, in their non-sovereign capacity, electing a new government. Crucially, at any time a citizenry may convene an emergency assembly to bring down a government that foisted bad regulations upon it despite its inability to strike down any individual decree formally. According to Rousseau, the sovereign assembly is legally barred from overruling or overturning any particular act of government because such interference is illegitimate and beyond its competency for wholly general matters.

Despite this legal impediment he also believes that the dominion of the people over their servants should be imposing or even fanglike in its silent control, terminally suspended like a sword of Damocles. A dull instrument in more traditional states, any impediment to sovereign power should be construed as being less of an impenetrable barrier to democratic transparency than as a movable obstacle in support of good governance. As a rule, no popular assembly should ever be held hostage to an incompetent or hostile executive. In most instances, of course, the assembly ought to be pleased with governmental affairs and plan to convene infrequently but, unfortunately, this is not always the case.[28]

MORALS, CUSTOMS AND OPINION

According to Rousseau, "morals, customs, and especially opinion" are central to the success of the laws. Imperceptibly substituting "the force of habit for that of authority," each of these three intangibles is what "the great Legislator attends to in secret while appearing to limit himself to the particular regulations that are merely the sides of the arch of which morals, slower to arise, form at last the unshakable Keystone" (CS, II:xii, 164–165/394).[29] Together, all three are the lynchpins to any successful legislation because they influence the basis and sustainability of individuals' identification with the common good.

Of the importance of morals, specifically, Rousseau's belief is that "the law acts externally and regulates only actions" but "morals alone penetrate internally and direct wills" (FP, XVI:vi, 71/555).

---

[28] Melzer writes that "Rousseau has in mind an old and conservative state living in more or less unchanging obedience to an ancient code inherited from a distant past when these laws were instituted by a heroic legislator and ratified by the people." As I explain in Chapters 2 and 6 the infrequency of meetings of the assembly in a truly well-ordered state should not be confused with political docility and passivity. This is especially true in light of the Genevan's example of republican Rome in which politics was marked by robustness, vibrancy and activity in contrast to a polity in which the people do nothing more than offer their silent acclammation or "unchanging obedience" to an old, conservative, inherited law code. See Melzer, The Natural Goodness of Man, 175.

[29] The whole of this famous passage reads: "A ces trois sortes de loix, il s'en joint une quatrieme, la plus importante de toutes; qui ne se grave ni sur le marbre ni sur l' airain, mais dans les coeurs des citoyens; qui fait la véritable constitution de l' Etat ... je parle des moeurs, des coutumes, et sur-tout de l' opinion; partie inconnue á nos politiques, mais de laquelle dépend le succès de toutes les autres."

The "greatest wellspring of public authority lies in the hearts of the citizens, and that for the maintenance of the government, nothing can replace good morals" (EP, 149/252). By "good morals," he means the Ciceronian concepts of civic pride, martial courage, a love of the *patrie*, etc., above any of the cardinal Christian virtues. His belief is that, unlike the Christian virtues of chastity, humility, self-sacrifice or mercy, it is the classical Roman or republican virtues that are essential to corporate unity and, more significantly, inculcating the psychological attributes that each must possess to resist the enslaving lure of *l'opinion*. Despite a vulnerability to *amour-propre*, individuals are able to withstand the machinations of the many and various *ennemis de l'opinion* because they are able to identify honor with the common good. Toward this end, salutary morals facilitate this process in a way that makes any differences between men's private and public wants indistinguishable. The distinctive traditions, mores, ethos and, especially, customs of a community help to direct morals in accordance with the common good.

According to the Genevan, it is communal customs that give temporal continuity to morals such that "the smallest change in customs ... always turns to the disadvantage of morals. For customs are the morality of the people" (N, 195/971). Any change is germane because whenever a people comes to "despise its customs, it soon finds the secret of eluding the laws" (N, 195/971). Over time, customs "preserve a people in the spirit of its institution" by giving this spirit a physicality that, together with salutary morals, impacts upon the laws.

Considering the primacy of this relationship between morals, customs and law, why Rousseau chooses to label public opinion also a part of the "genuine constitution of the state" is not especially clear. Of this, scholars such as Jürgen Habermas, Mona Ozouf, Keith Michael Baker and J.A.W. Gunn believe that Rousseau articulates an unusually apolitical version of the modern eighteenth-century concept of *l'opinion publique* as a legitimizing force to democracy. According to Habermas, for example, Rousseau's construct is said to be "unpublic opinion," or an uncritical, undeliberative general will.[30] In the *Social Contract*, "unpublic opinion was elevated to the status of sole legislator, and this involved the elimination of the public's rational-critical debate in the public sphere." Habermas describes Rousseau as using the prefix "public" to emphasize the people's presence during voting rather than to illustrate the openness or "publicness" of their opinions. For the Genevan, "a direct democracy required that the sovereign be actually present. The general will as the *corpus mysticum* was bound up with the corpus physicum of the people as a consensual assembly."[31] Critically, Habermas rejects Rousseau as an innovator of the modern concept

[30] Jürgen Habermas, *The Structural Transformation of the Public Sphere: An Inquiry Into a Category of Bourgeois Society*, trans. Thomas Burger and Fredrick Lawrence, Cambridge, MA: MIT Press, 1989 [1962], 90, 97, 99. Arguably, this reading by Habermas is overly narrow. It is important to remember that Rousseau's definition of *l'opinion publique* extends beyond *la volonté générale* in his political writings. Each construct is administered by two separate executives in his state. He writes that "public opinion is the kind of law of which the Censor is the Minister, and which he only applies to particular situations, following the example of the Prince" (*CS*, IV:vii, 214/458). Likewise, elsewhere he contrasts "the force of the laws" to "the empire of opinion" in his *Letter to Alembert*. He writes that "I know of only three instruments with which the morals of a people can be acted upon: the force of laws, the empire of opinion, and the appeal of pleasure" (*LA*, 266/20–21). The force of the laws and the empire of opinion are two distinct types of influence that impinge upon morals. Each converges when the laws shape and guide opinion by way of censorship.

I am grateful to Bernard Manin for highlighting these differences to me. Habermas, of course, is *not* a Rousseau scholar but his views are relevant on this question owing to their impact on Rousseau scholarship as well as his enormous influence in sociology and political science. In Allesandro Ferraro's book on Rousseau, *Modernity and Authenticity*, for example, the author follows Habermas' reading of the *Social Contract* on this question. Prior to Habermas' book, Hans Speier comments that "Rousseau put public opinion in its modern political place, demanding that the law should spring from the general will." Earlier, Leo Strauss describes Rousseauian *l'opinion* as "the standard of free society," a standard questionable from a "transpolitical point of view." See Allesandro Ferrara, *Modernity and Authenticity*, New York: SUNY Press, 1993, 59; Hans Speier, "The Historical Development of Public Opinion," *American Journal of Sociology*, LV, July 1949–May 1950, 378; Leo Strauss, "On the Intention of Rousseau," *Social Research*, XIV, December 1947, 473.

[31] Habermas, *The Structural Transformation of the Public Sphere*, 90, 97, 99. Since the publication some fifty years ago of Jürgen Habermas' seminal study *The Structural Transformation of the Public Sphere* (1962) the history and the

of *l'opinion publique* because, unlike his rationalist Enlightenment contemporaries, his few uses of the term in his political writings refer explicitly to the judgments of an uncritical and non-deliberative majority rather than to the judgments by a literate public engaging in critical open debate.[32]

historiography of the term "public opinion" have been subjects of controversy. Today, little consensus exists over whether England or France is the birthplace of "public opinion" and which first appearance of the term ought to be considered modern in the sense of connoting a meaning other than superstition, emotion or Platonic *doxa*. Some authors cite openness or publicity as the concept's most distinguishing feature while others emphasize its political character or ability to legitimate claims by competing political actors. The term "public opinion" may connote either political opinion, expressly, or a public space where an independent and enlightened citizen-body engages in rational discourse on any variety of topics. Although this first definition is contingent upon the second many European historians reject the sociological definition as overly general.

[32] More than anything else, what distinguishes the modern eighteenth-century concept of "public opinion" from the archaic notion of Platonic *doxa*, is *raison*. As pre- and post-Revolutionary literati such as Voltaire, Necker and Condorcet hypothesized, it is the leveling power of reason alone that universalizes a plurality of atomistic individuals into an enlightened tribunal that is capable of exercising political authority. Public opinion is critical and deliberative rather than arbitrary and speculative.

Keith Michael Baker remarks that the eighteenth-century definitional reconfiguration of the term "*l'opinion*" into "*l'opinion publique*" was employed as a rhetorical weapon against the *ancien régime* in France in a way that coincided with the sociological emergence of what Jürgen Habermas famously terms "the public sphere" (assuming such a bracketed discursive space ever existed). Within the corridors of Westminster and France's National Assembly, those who spoke of "public opinion" did so aware of the conjoined term's extraordinary rhetorical sway. Among other writings, between 1760 and 1790, this new literary invention appeared in the economic and philosophical writings of Physiocratic thinkers such as Necker, Turgot, Duclos, Raynal, Condorcet and, after 1800, the political tracts of Constant and Guizot.

Pointedly absent from this coterie of intellectual innovators is Rousseau. Although, Rousseau, Constant and Guizot each use the same modern term "*l'opinion publique*," only the two latter thinkers are said to employ it in a modern way. In recent years this pre-modern view of Rousseau's construct has received auspicious support by the British historian J.A.W. Gunn who argues that whatever political content that Rousseau ascribes to his concept of "*l' opinion publique*" is indistinguishable from Platonic *doxa*, or vain sentiments, prejudices and emotion. Gunn writes that, for Rousseau, "it is the problem of the public, and not the solution, that is most prominent:" opinion is most relevant and interesting to the social and political problems it creates, not to any solution it might offer. Gunn criticizes commentators who date or place the term's origin by non-political criteria writing that "certain factors have been responsible for the uncritical assumption that writers were dealing with public

Likewise, according to Mona Ozouf, across his many books, discourses and letters, Rousseau is said to employ the term *l'opinion publique* but with a definition that is too anachronistically subjective or sentimental to possess a "polemical charge."[33] It is the capriciousness, unpredictability and variability that the Genevan associates with the construct that is said to undermine his intellectual contribution. In light of this concept's significance to his political thought it is worthwhile to examine why Rousseau considers opinion to be a part of a "fourth law" of which the "success of all the others depends" (*CS*, II:xii, 165/394).

THE PSYCHOLOGY OF OPINION

One of the most crystalline statements on the relationship between law and opinion can be found in a short missive that was sent by Rousseau

opinion when in fact they had no intention of discussing the modern phenomenon. Sometimes this has been the result ... from paying too much attention to the exact words 'public opinion,' without inquiring about the meaning that was being attached to them."

It is noteworthy that this reading by Baker, Habermas and Gunn is disputed by the German sociologist Elisabeth Noëlle-Neumann. According to Noëlle-Neumann, Rousseau ought to be considered the originator or "father" of the modern concept of public opinion. This original distinction, specifically locating the evolution of the modern concept in the writings of Enlightenment thinkers from pre- and post-Revolutionary France, credits Rousseau with "inventing" the phrase by his very early and repeated use of the conjoined term *l'opinion publique*. Unlike earlier European thinkers who used only the singular term *"l'opinion"* or, like Montaigne and Pascal, applied the conjoined term only in select places, Rousseau is said to be unique for repeating the modern phrase across a variety of works dating back as early as the 1740s and – critically – describing opinion as a species of law. See Keith Michael Baker, *Inventing the French Revolution: Essays on French Political Culture in the Eighteenth Century*, Cambridge and London: Cambridge University Press, 1990, 167–199; J.A.W. Gunn, *Queen of the World: Opinion in the Public Life of France from the Renaissance to the Revolution*, Voltaire Foundation, Oxford: Alden Press, 1995, 180; *Beyond Liberty and Property: the Process of Self-recognition in Eighteenth Century Political Thought*, Kingston and Montreal: McGill-Queen's University Press, 1985, 261, 265–266; Elisabeth Noëlle-Neumann, *The Spiral of Silence: Our Social Skin*, Chicago: The University of Chicago Press, 1984, 80–87.

[33] Mona Ozouf, "Public Spirit," in *A Critical Dictionary of the French Revolution*, ed. F. Furet and M. Ozouf, trans. A. Goldhammer, Cambridge, MA: Belknap Press, Harvard University Press, 1989, 772; also see Ozouf, "'Public Opinion' at the End of the Old Regime," *Journal of Modern History* 60, suppl., September 1988, S4–S9.

to Mirabeau on July 26, 1767, thanking the revolutionary-in-waiting for delivering a copy of Mercier de la Riviere's *Natural and Essential Order of Political Societies* (1767) to him. In this letter Rousseau responds to Riviere's optimism in the possibility of society being governed by rationally demonstrable principles, asking "what is the use of reason enlightening us if it is passion that leads us?" Rejecting the Physiocrat's assumption that European despots would find common ground with their subjects in the *évidence* of rationally enlightened truth, he claims "that each of us acts very rarely on his knowledge and very often according to his passions."[34] Rousseau asserts that rationally enlightened truth can never emerge from the morass of opinion because reason will always be conquered by prejudice. Even if "reason shows us the goal" the "passions divert us from it" (*N*, 188/962). *L'évidence* or the idea of *rational opinion*, so to speak, is an oxymoron.

Unlike other French thinkers prior to 1789, such as Turgot, Necker, Duclos and Peuchet, or post-Revolutionary authors such as Constant and Guizot, Rousseau emphasizes the primacy of the passions and, especially, prejudice to this "fourth law." It is his belief that neither reason nor violence can dominate opinion effectively and, vitally, during the occasions when the latter clashes with the laws there can be no warning of punishment because "neither sword nor fire nor the whip of court Pedants can make that precept observed" (*FP*, IV:vii, 29/493). Frequent resort to violence is not only politically illegitimate but impotent as a long-term tool of the state. Rather, it is not violence but morals, customs and opinion that are the bulwarks of the laws and each must be carefully guided or "refashioned" in order to reinforce the latter's coercive power.

Unlike Montesquieu's description of opinion in Book XIX of *The Spirit of the Laws*, Rousseau's use of the term "*l'opinion*" can be argued to be an original and indeed an intellectual contribution to the history of political thought owing to the autonomy that he

---

[34] *Letter to M. le marquis de Mirabeau* (26 July 1767), in Jean-Jacques Rousseau, *Citizen of Geneva: Selections from the Letters*, ed. C.W. Hendel, Oxford: Oxford University Press, 1937, 160.

attributes to the construct. The added weight of "above all opinion" ("*sur-tout de l' opinion*") when referring to the laws, specifically, illuminates his cognizance of the distinctiveness and modernity of his usage of the term. Legislators should be highly circumspect of opinion *above all* because it is, at root, "difficult to govern" (*LA*, 305/68) and an unruly power that is uncontrollable by conventional means. Violence is sometimes a legitimate, albeit ineffective, tool of the laws but never when its object is public opinion. Any attempt at coercion in this direction is mistaken even if violence is defensible in other limited circumstances, according to Rousseau (*EP*, 150/253–254; *CGP*, III, 179/965).[35]

Similar to its resistance to violence, opinion is also inordinately difficult to influence or manipulate by way of reason. In his *Letter to Alembert*, he describes this resistance as, perhaps, the concept's most salient political trait. "Very mobile and changing," it is always the case with opinion that "chance, countless accidental causes, countless unforeseen circumstances, do what force and reason could not." It is "precisely because chance directs them that force can do nothing; like the dice which leaves the hand, whatever impulsion is given them does not bring up the desired point more easily" (*LA*, 305/68).[36]

---

[35] Rousseau does not reject the sword as a means to enforcing the laws, but he recognizes its uselessness when laws and opinion clash. In cases where there is no contradiction between opinion and the laws force may prove effective. People will respond to the sword because loss of esteem is not an issue. In this regard, the prince requires the censor's help only when the laws possibly contradict public opinion (or vice versa) or as a preventative measure for ensuring opinion and the laws remain harmonious. As I discuss in Chapter 5, his assumptions about human nature establish this contradiction and frequent clashes between opinion and the laws to be more the *rule* than the exception. In *Corsica* Rousseau describes the utility of force as limited, short-term expedient for curtailing certain behaviors without eliminating them. He sees coercion as beneficial to the laws by its capacity to *restrain* but never *compel*. It is useful as a negative sanction only, never a positive stimulus for action. The fear of punishment is an exclusively negative power and persons will never act from fear but only cease to act. I also discuss this below. See *Corsica*, 325/937.

[36] Rousseau speaks of "whatever impulsion is given them" because *l'opinion publique* is a pluralized rather than a unitary construct in his writings. This

In this passage, opinion's vulnerability to "unforeseen circumstances" is said to give it a randomness, fickleness or variability that makes it unpredictable. Persons "drift from whim to whim" with their "tastes being constantly enslaved to opinion" (*JNH*, II:xvii, 209/255) above all else. In the *Reveries*, the Genevan attributes the cause of this to man's natural passions transmogrified by contemporary society into *amour-propre* and prejudice, for

> the judgments of the public are quite often equitable. But I
> did not see that this very equity was the effect of chance, that
> the rules on which they base their opinions are drawn only
> from their passions or their prejudices, which are the work of
> their passions, and that even when they judge well, these good
> judgments still frequently arise from a bad principle.
>
> (RPS, VIII, 71/1077)[37]

archaic definition of the construct was altered radically under the pen of Voltaire, Condorcet and others during the 1780s. Ozouf points to the appearance of this pluralized term, "*l'opinion publiques*," as evidence of its particularized or apolitical status for Rousseau. Instead of articulating a self-evident, objective and unitary public voice, the philosopher offers a mostly fractious and particular amalgam of arbitrary sentiments and emotions. But these attributes are what make it politically relevant. See Ozouf, "'Public Opinion' at the End of the Old Regime," S3.

[37] As all are aware, the Genevan's famous claim that "it is passion that leads us" is one of the most transcendent ideas in his political writings and in his corpus generally. In one form or another this idea appears in many of his key writings (*DI*, I, 27/143; *E*, II, 80–81/304–305; *FP*, XVI:i, 70/554; *N*, 188/962) and often in express reference to opinion (*LA*, 300/62; *CS*, IV, vii, 215/458; *CGP*, 175–176/961; *PC*, 153/937; *RPS*, VIII, 71/1077). Rejecting the ancients' equating of human essence with reason, he builds upon the later beliefs of Hobbes, Hume and others who argue that the purpose of reason is to facilitate the passions (*DI*, I, 116/143; *E*, II, 80–81/304–305; *FP*, XVI:i, 70/554). It is his view that persons seek knowledge only to fulfill pleasure and man "consults solely his passions in order to act ... reason serves only to palliate the follies his passions led him to commit" (*FP*, XVI:i, 70/554).

Of all of the human senses, vision and hearing exert the greatest bearing upon the passions and, by extension, the formation of opinion owing to how individuals process information, according to Rousseau. Although in *Emile* he emphasizes the primacy of man's sensitivity to tactile sensation, in the *Essay on the Origin of Languages* he emphasizes the superior power of sight and hearing upon human cognition. Each is said to affect human emotion differently according to their distinct modes of process. Sight arouses emotion directly where sound is mediated by imagination. This mediation does not

Arguably, in the *Social Contract* it is this reworking or rede-
fining of the Platonic concept of *doxa* that can be shown to distinguish Rousseau's usage from those of his ancient predecessors
and eighteenth-century contemporaries. Unlike *doxa* or "things
taken for granted as part of a culture, normative convictions, collective prejudices and judgments," his concept resists force and reason to erect inviolable boundaries. There are some things to which
opinion gives continuous restraint and it is its opposition to *raison*
that transports it beyond the earlier accepted categories relating
to traditional political authority. Significantly, Rousseau refers
to the concept's opposition to government explicitly ("difficult to
govern") leaving no doubt that his unique rendering is intended
to spotlight a quasi-autonomous locus of political power inside of
a conventional state. Rejecting Pascal's assertion that "opinion is
queen of the world and force is her king,"[38] he writes instead that

> involve reason or intellect but imagination exclusively. The principal pleasure
> of sound emanates from its effects upon imagination and the images that it
> evokes within the mind. Sound inspires memory, fantasy, reverie and a host
> of mental imagery originally imparted (elementally) by sight. Sight imparts
> impressions which hearing recreates as imaginative visual representations.
> In this regard, music, for example, touches persons on a visceral level by
> inspiring emotions that redouble the power of all of the other senses. Sound
> multiplies the power of sight, for example, by creating aural imagery mimick-
> ing sight; sounds "never have more energy than when they produce the effect
> of colors" (*EOL*, I, 291/377; XVI, 326/420–421).
>
> Likewise, visual imagery affects opinion by stimulating men's emotions at
> a more physical level. Sight arouses excitement, joy, fear, envy and a host of
> emotions directly, immediately, and with reference to nothing. This is evident
> in spectators' reactions to colorful imagery and its ability to elicit sadness,
> stifle anger, or elate. Unlike hearing which moves men by representation
> exclusively, sight inspires emotion through imitation and is the most honest
> form of persuasion. In this respect, public opinion is less likely to be deceived
> by visual spectacle than by reason or the other senses because its impact is
> immediate. Individuals alternatively respond to or ignore different types
> of impressions but are unable to delay their reactions to reflect upon their
> representations. Unlike music or even isolated sounds, visual imagery creates
> instantaneous impressions or falls flat. This brevity explains why arbiters of
> opinion resort to reasoning, rationalization, "deadly paradox," and long-term
> sensations, such as a theater performance.
>
> [38] "L'empire fondé sur l'opinion et l'imagination règne quelque temps, et cet
> empire est doux et volontaire; celui de la force règne toujours. Ainsi l'opinion

"Opinion, queen of the world, is not subject to the power of kings; they are themselves her first slaves." Opinion does "what force and reason could not" as "nothing is more independent of the supreme power than the judgment of the public."[39] This original construct, more sweeping than Constant's "magic circle,"[40] spins its own web around absolute sovereignty by its effect upon the laws. Two decades before Jacques Necker acknowledges the salience of this trait in his writings on public finance, Rousseau not only discusses but *analyzes* the psychology and political implications of government's dependency on opinion.[41] He explains that no serious political thinker can ignore the "Queen of the World" owing to its unruly coercive power.

LAW AND LEGISLATION IN THE *SOCIAL CONTRACT*

Law, morals, customs and opinion are central to the program of the *Social Contract*. More than being relevant to "the conditions of the civil association," each is best understood in relation to Rousseau's ideas about "universal justice," procedural equity, sovereignty and

---

est comme la reine du monde, mais la force en est le tyran." *Pensées de Blaise Pascal*, ed. Leon Brunschvigg, Librairie Générale Française, Paris, 1972 (No. 311), 149.

[39] *Letter to Alembert*, 301/63.

[40] See B. Fontana, *Benjamin Constant and the Post Revolutionary Mind*, London and New Haven: Yale University Press, 1991, 83; originally in Constant, *Fragments d'un ouvrage abandonné sur la possibilité d'une constitution républicaine dans un grand Pays*, Naf. 14363, fol. 66b. Also see Stephen Holmes' view of opinion in Constant's writings in *Benjamin Constant and the Origins of Modern Liberalism*, London and New Haven: Yale University Press, 1984.

[41] Similar to Rousseau's view of the dependency of the laws on opinion, David Hume believes that opinion is indispensable to military and state power. It is noteworthy that he expresses this notion decades before Voltaire or Necker and slightly ahead of Rousseau. Hume proclaims that it is "on opinion only that government is founded; and this maxim extends to the most despotic and most military governments, as well as to the most free and most popular. The soldan of Egypt, or the Emperor of Rome, might drive his harmless subjects, like brute beasts, against their sentiments and inclination: but he must, at least, have led his mamalukes, or praetorian bands, like men, by their opinions." See David Hume, *Essays Moral, Political, and Literary*, ed. Eugene F. Miller, Indianapolis: Liberty Press, 1985 [1742], "Of the First Principles of Government," 32–33.

statecraft, more generally. As I will discuss in the following chapters, the starting point for this range of ideas is the agenda-setting process that precedes ratification. As an inseparable unity, each of the three activities of *drafting, ratifying* and *executing* determines whether the laws can be considered just and whether or not the people as a whole can be considered free.

2 Agenda-setting and majority rule

According to Carole Pateman a central tenet of "strong democracy" and other contemporary theories of participatory democracy is the belief that the "more that individuals participate" in self-governance "the better able they become to do so."[1] More valuable than expert guidance by an elected elite is the political education received from democratic participation under conditions of political equality. Knowledge of how to govern is "communal and consensual" and through the holding of televised debates, town hall meetings, referendums, plebiscites, open ballot initiatives and other practical expressions of citizen self-rule, the people "deepen" the quality of democracy by expressing their will directly. Although the people may lack certain forms of specialized knowledge and technical skill, over time this void will be filled because "the pragmatic and self-regulating character of democratic politics" makes "political knowledge autonomous."[2] Challenging this view, twentieth-century critics of participatory democracy routinely emphasize government's need for specialized competency and legislative expertise.[3] They argue that it is impractical, if not utopian, to believe that a majority can or should legislate the laws without critical intervention by experts. Requisite for overcoming the logistical difficulties of size and numbers, agenda-setting by a professional body or class of legislators

---

[1] Carole Pateman, *Participation and Democratic Theory*, Cambridge: Cambridge University Press, 1970, 43. Also see Joel D. Wolfe, "A Defense of Participatory Democracy," *The Review of Politics* 47 (3) 1985: 371; Benjamin R. Barber, *Strong Democracy: Participatory Politics for a New Age*, Berkeley: University of California Press, 1985, 167–173.

[2] Barber, *Strong Democracy*, 167.

[3] Giovanni Sartori, *The Theory of Democracy Revisited*, Part II, Chatham: Chatham House, 1987, 432; Joseph A. Schumpeter, *Capitalism, Socialism and Democracy*, London: Allen and Unwin, 1943, 261–262.

makes possible enlightened lawmaking. As Thomas Hobbes wrote back in 1642, "very few in a great Assembly of men understand" by "what goods the Country is nourished, and defended" or are able "to advise rightly of all things conducing to the preservation of a Common-weal."[4]

Both of these contrary viewpoints allude to a dilemma unique to representative government in which those persons who are most able to advance and benefit the aspirations of the people by way of their specialized knowledge are simultaneously those also most capable and likely to undermine majority rule. This dilemma exists even in a participatory democracy because, as John Stuart Mill noted, the political value of participation mitigates but does not entirely diminish government's need for lawmaking professionals.[5] Identifying the basis of this dilemma, Robert Michels wrote a half century later, "this special competence, this expert knowledge, which the leader acquires in matters inaccessible, or almost inaccessible, to the mass ... conflicts with the essential principles of democracy."[6] Similarly, Hanna F. Pitkin explains in her classic study "whenever we seek professional help or services, we are asking to be represented" for "the presumption of a specialized knowledge or skill in the representative suggests that he need not take orders from his constituents." This suggestion that representatives "need not take orders from his constituents" is not illegitimate because it is "the presumption of a specialized knowledge or skill" in representatives that, in part, is the source of their authority.[7] This said, democracy's dilemma remains in that experts elected to serve beneath the people may surreptitiously serve over them by applying this specialized knowledge in a manner designed to keep those who selected them

---

[4] Thomas Hobbes, *The English Works of Thomas Hobbes of Malmesbury*, ed. Sir W. Molesworth, vol. II, London: John Bohn, 1841 [1642], *De Cive*, X:x, 136–137.

[5] John Stuart Mill, "Considerations on Representative Government," in *Three Essays*, Oxford: Oxford University Press, 1975 [1861], 223.

[6] Robert Michels, *Political Parties: A Sociological Study of the Oligarchical Tendencies of Modern Democracy*, Glencoe, IL: The Free Press, 1915, 83–84.

[7] Hanna Fenichel Pitkin, *The Concept of Representation*, Berkeley: University of California Press, 1967, 135–136.

in ignorance of their actual situation. As has often been the case in history, experts have even utilized their knowledge in a manner that violates the rights and freedoms that give democracy meaning. Considering this danger, it is meaningful to ask whether agenda-setting by experts and majority rule must *necessarily* conflict in the way that these theorists describe. Is it true that whenever democrats authorize experts to agenda-set the laws they are indeed "asking to be represented"?

One answer to this question was voiced many years ago by the earliest and, perhaps, the most radical proponent of participatory democracy ever, Jean-Jacques Rousseau. In his political writings, Rousseau argues that majority rule is indeed possible even in the presence of agenda-setting experts. By "majority rule," I mean, specifically, rule by the people in the broadest sense of the term as active, influential and practically meaningful participation in lawmaking even when experts set the agenda. By this term I also mean, temporally, lawmaking after the foundational lawgiver of Rousseau's *Social Contract* voluntarily cedes its authority to the citizenry and to those persons among them who will assume its functions. This expansion of self-rule, dealt with parsimoniously in the vast literature on the *Social Contract*, begins when citizens are mature enough morally and politically to be able to comprehend and institutionalize the general will free of paternalistic interference by the lawgiver. Lasting for a number of years, presumably, before the inevitable decline of the republic owing to the debasement of public morals, this era of (at least formally) unmediated self-governance is a time when the laws appear to be most democratic.

It is also the moment when, according to Steven Johnston, Daniel Cullen and Richard Fralin,[8] among other authors, the representative features in Rousseau's complex system come most into

---

[8] Johnston and Cullen echo Richard Fralin's once-controversial view that elected aristocrats are the decisive legislative figures in Rousseau's state. In *Rousseau and Representation* (1978), Fralin argues that Rousseau consolidates legislative power in the hands of an elected elite in much the same way that Geneva's *petit Conseil* pre-decided all legislation put before the ratifying *Conseil général*.

play as the authority to initiate the laws devolves from the lawgiver to a select body of elected aristocrats whose job it is to pre-decide all legislation to be put before the people's vote (*CS*, III:v, 175/408).[9] According to these commentators, this crucial agenda-setting role undermines majority rule by elevating elected representatives into a locus of legislative authority in Rousseau's mature state. Johnston writes, for example, that with the ratification of the laws "will masquerades as a property of the sovereign realm [as] government assumes responsibility for its actual formation and maintenance."[10] In Rousseau's state "the subject-citizen" is a "contrivance of power" and an "artifice to be constructed more than an essence to be realized."[11] Less harshly, Cullen explains that in Rousseau's polity the initiation of law by representatives reduces the people to "passivity" and "a punctuation of the political process."[12]

This view is similar to that of Roger D. Masters and the late Judith N. Shklar whom, years earlier, argued that government exerts

Fralin writes "the model of the *Contrat social* was ... recognizably the same basic model as that of the *Dédicace*" [to the Second *Discours* – where Rousseau extols the sagacity of Geneva's *petit Conseil* and warns of the dangers of majoritarian self-rule]. Within Geneva "the allegedly subordinate councils were superior in fact; not only was there not an identity of interests among citizens, but the city was in effect divided into separate bodies, each contending for power." See Steven Johnston, *Encountering Tragedy: Rousseau and the Project of Democratic Order*, Ithaca: Cornell University Press, 1999, 87, 118; D.E. Cullen, *Freedom in Rousseau's Political Philosophy*, De Kalb: Northern Illinois University Press, 1993, 152–153; Richard Fralin, *Rousseau and Representation: a Study of the Development of his Concept of Political Institutions*, New York: Columbia University Press, 1978, 54.

9 Rousseau writes in the *Social Contract* that "Sovereignty cannot be represented for the same reason it cannot be alienated. It consists essentially in the general will and the will cannot be represented. Either it is itself or it is something else; there is no middle ground. The deputies of the people, therefore, are not nor can they be its representatives; they are merely its agents [*commissaires*]. They cannot conclude anything definitively" (*CS*, III:xv, 192/429–430). In the only other section of the treatise where he discusses legislative initiation in his mature state, Rousseau writes that "on the right to give an opinion, to make propositions, to analyze, to discuss, which the Government is always very careful to allow only to its members" (*CS*, IV:i, 199/439).

10 Johnston, *Encountering Tragedy*, 87.

11 Johnston, *Encountering Tragedy*, 87.

12 Cullen, *Freedom in Rousseau's Political Philosophy*, 152–153.

far more influence in Rousseau's state than is apparent from the philosopher's denunciations of representation. Each concurred with Giovanni Sartori's (later) description of representatives as serving to mobilize an otherwise "immobile democracy."[13] Owing to the generality of its vote, the infrequency of its meetings and Rousseau's requirement that laws pertain solely to the "conditions of the civil association," Shklar concludes that "the sovereign does very little."[14] Masters writes that, in the past, the philosopher's "explicit preference for elective aristocracy has not been sufficiently considered ... [as it is] merely another name for parliamentary or representative government."[15] Johnston agrees that "if Rousseau's texts are read carefully, I would suggest, the prominence of law and politics recede somewhat and the importance of government surges," and he asks "Are such subjects really capable of sovereign responsibility? Of changing entrenched laws, whether the best or the worst?"[16]

This seemingly narrow question about the locus of political authority in Rousseau's state is relevant to more contemporary theories of participatory democracy by reinforcing the Schumpeterian view that democracy is rule by elites. Rousseau's sovereign is "constructed" in the sense that Schumpeter believes that politicians "fashion and ... create the will of the people" into a "manufactured will."[17] His constructed sovereign is seen as incapable of either self-imposed law or of self-reinforcing government. If Rousseau is viewed as the "theorist *par excellence* of participation"[18] whose republican ideas are "the most radical, if not the most radical, ever developed,"[19] as David Held describes, this is a particularly forceful and pointed criticism. In a different vein, this criticism of the philosopher highlights a problem of

[13] Sartori, *The Theory of Democracy Revisited*, 314.

[14] Judith N. Shklar, *Men and Citizens: A Study of Rousseau's Social Theory*, Cambridge and New York: Cambridge University Press, 1987 [1969], 181.

[15] Roger D. Masters, *The Political Philosophy of Rousseau*, Princeton: Princeton University Press, 1968, 402.

[16] Johnston, *Encountering Tragedy*, 118.

[17] Schumpeter, *Capitalism, Socialism and Democracy*, 262, 263.

[18] Pateman, *Participation and Democratic Theory*, 22.

[19] David Held, *Theories of Democracy*, London: Blackwell, 1996, 56.

legislative agenda-setting, generally, that "citizens of Western democracies can vote for those who will govern them but rarely for the policies by which they are governed; more rarely are they provided the opportunity to create their own agendas through permanent public discourse."[20] Rousseau appears unable to reconcile democracy's dual needs of expert agenda-setting and majority rule in even a minimalist system in which "permanent public discourse" is not an issue.

It is my view that Rousseau neither intends nor does his constitutional plan allow for representation in any strong sense. Rejecting Shklar's belief that "the sovereign does very little," it is possible to argue that democracy in his mature state is more robust than appears owing to a number of institutional and other substantive checks designed to prevent sovereignty being reduced to a mere "punctuation of the political process." In a similar vein, it is possible to show that the alternative overly democratic or populist reading of lawmaking in his state is also wanting to the extent that this interpretation fails to explain why Rousseau permits a body other than the sovereign to participate in legislative agenda-setting. If men are as ripe for self-rule as he implies then why is a separation of powers among lawmakers even necessary? To answer this question adequately one must begin by locating the source of the constitutional laws in Rousseau's just state. More specifically, it is necessary to identify the body responsible for agenda-setting after the foundational lawgiver departs to what the Genevan calls his "future glory" in "the passage of time."

LOCATING LEGISLATIVE AGENDA-SETTING IN THE *SOCIAL CONTRACT*

Who drafts the laws in Rousseau's state? This question, together with the more salient one of how legislation ought to be drafted, has been a subject of controversy within the secondary literature on the political theory of the *Social Contract* for many decades. During this

---

[20] Barber, *Strong Democracy*, 267.

time, there has been a wide divide in the scholarship over whether
it is the people in conjunction with experts who draft the laws or
whether it is the sovereign alone who assumes this vital function.
For the most part, this division is between those commentators who
believe that the philosopher ascribes this duty to the people alone
and those who describe legislative agenda-setting as a joint function between the sovereign and governmental experts.[21] Separating
these two viewpoints, it is possible to demonstrate that it is the latter rather than the former that best conforms to Rousseau's view of
lawmaking in a just state.

[21] According to John T. Scott, N.J.H. Dent, Stephen Ellenburg and some early
twentieth-century readers like Cobban and Vaughan, it is the sovereign
who inherits the lawgiver's duty of initiating the laws in Rousseau's state
(John T. Scott, "Rousseau's Anti-Agenda-Setting Agenda and Contemporary
Democratic Theory," *American Political Science Review* 99 (1) 2005: 137–144;
James Miller, *Rousseau: Dreamer of Democracy*, New Haven: Yale University
Press, 1984, 64; N.J.H. Dent, *Rousseau: An Introduction to his Psychological,
Social and Political Theory*, London: Blackwell, 1988, 172; Stephen Ellenburg,
Rousseau's Political Philosophy: An Interpretation from within, Ithaca: Cornell
University Press, 1976, 159–160; Alfred Cobban, *Rousseau and the Modern
State*, London: Allen and Unwin, 1934, 91; C.E. Vaughan, *The Political Writings
of Jean-Jacques Rousseau*, vol. I and II, Cambridge: Cambridge University
Press, 1915, 187). For a number of others, such as Melzer, Gildin and Masters,
it is the government that inherits the bulk of this responsibility (M. Qvortrup,
*The Political Philosophy of Jean-Jacques Rousseau: The Impossibility of
Reason*, Manchester and New York: Manchester University Press, 2003, 57–58;
D.E. Cullen, *Freedom in Rousseau's Political Philosophy*, De Kalb: Northern
Illinois University Press, 1993, 152; Arthur M. Melzer, *The Natural Goodness
of Man: On the System of Rousseau's Thought*, Chicago: The University of
Chicago Press, 1990, 237; J. Cohen, "Reflections on Rousseau: Autonomy and
Democracy," *Philosophy and Public Affairs*, 15 (3) 1986, 295–296; H. Gildin,
Rousseau's Social Contract: the Design of the Argument, Chicago: The
University of Chicago Press, 1983, 159; R.D. Masters, *The Political Philosophy
of Rousseau*, Princeton: Princeton University Press, 1968, 402). Melzer writes,
for example, that Rousseau gives the government "not only the executive power
but also a part of the legislative power (without calling it that): the power of
convening the assembly and of legislative initiative. From this fact alone it is
obvious that the Government will not simply execute the sovereign's laws as
its mere agent, but will have an enormous power to influence or manipulate the
outcome of the sovereign assembly" (*The Natural Goodness of Man*, 237).
Vaughan claims that while "there is nothing expressly contrary" to the notion
of agenda-setting by a body other than the sovereign, such a possibility is contradictory to "the whole spirit" of Rousseau's political philosophy. "If the sovereign body is not entitled to consider and pass any law but those prepared and

Arguably, there are at least three good reasons for concluding that it is the people who draft the laws unassisted in Rousseau's state. Of these three reasons, the first two place great emphasis upon the indivisibility of sovereign power. The third highlights the self-control or self-discipline of an assembly that is well-ordered. Of the first, Rousseau writes that any time that the government shares in legislation the result is an illegitimate division of sovereignty (*EP*, 142/244; *CS*, III:i, 166/395; III:iv, 173/404; *LEM*, IV, 232/808). Any time that the government engages in lawmaking it necessarily violates the functional separation between legislation and execution that must be honored for the laws to stay general. As a wider danger, his belief is that whatever benefits the state might reap from agenda-setting by government will be undermined ultimately by its members' insatiable drive for power. "It would be sheer madness," according to the philosopher, "to hope that those

put before it by the Executive," Vaughan writes, "then the sovereign is no longer sovereign; the Executive is its master. The right to initiate laws is as much a necessary part of the legislative power as the right to control their execution. Without the one, as without the other, the 'right of Legislation' is a fraud" (*The Political Writings of Jean-Jacques Rousseau*, II, 187). Much more recently, Scott claims the philosopher "nowhere positively argues that the government should possess the right to propose laws" or that "when he seems to acknowledge such a right" in his *Dedicatory Letter* to the *Second Discourse* and *Letters Written from the Mountain* "he is trying to limit the damage from what he otherwise considers an illegitimate arrangement" ("Rousseau's Anti-Agenda-Setting Agenda," 141).

Offering an alternative viewpoint, Masters asserts "Rousseau expected that the laws would be prepared for popular enactment by representatives" (*The Political Philosophy of Rousseau*, 402). Gildin's belief is that "Rousseau undoubtedly affirms that the right to vote on laws cannot be taken from the citizens. He undoubtedly makes no such affirmation about the right to propose and debate them" (*Rousseau's Social Contract*, 159). Similarly, Fralin writes, "Rousseau does not provide for a popular legislative initiative in the *Contrat Social* ... not only does Rousseau fail to provide for a popular legislative initiative in the assembly, but he also specifically prohibits the people from calling a meeting of the assembly on their own initiative" (*Rousseau and Representation*, 107–108). Unlike these commentators, Melzer takes a middle road on the question: Rousseau is "noncommittal" about the question of "who shall have the right to initiate legislation and the right to speak before the assembly" (*The Natural Goodness of Man*, 173), arguing that the philosopher's "preference" is for legislation to be proposed by magistrates but with the "right to debate" belonging "to all."

who are in fact masters will prefer another interest to their own" (*EP*, 145/247).

In the seventh and eighth of his *Letters Written from the Mountain*, Rousseau offers his most positive statements on popular agenda-setting. Speaking of the people (or the closest thing to it, the *Conseil général*) he writes that "it is up to the Legislator, it is up to the drafter of the Laws not to leave equivocal terms in them. When they are there, it is up to the equity of the Magistrate to fix them in practice" (*LEM*, VIII, 277/862). More sharply, he asks "isn't it contrary to all reason that the executive body rule the public order of the Legislative body, that it prescribe to it the matters it must take cognizance of, that it forbid it the right of giving an opinion, and that it exercise its absolute power even in the acts made to hold it within limits?" (*LEM*, VII, 251/830).

A second reason for concluding that Rousseau's laws are drafted by the people alone is that "to the degree that it becomes necessary to promulgate new ones [laws], this necessity is universally seen" (*CS*, IV:i, 198/437). In a just state such guidance by an elite is unnecessary because "all the mechanisms of the State are vigorous and simple, its maxims are clear and luminous, it has no tangled or contradictory interests; the common good is clearly apparent everywhere, and requires only good sense to be perceived" (*CS*, IV:i, 198/437). The people do not need legislative experts because the majority knows what it wants and has no "tangled or contradictory interests." With such a heightened degree of clarity each citizen would not "propose new Laws according to his fancy" (*DI*, 5/114) but according to universally shared conceptions of right. This is possible because citizens raised in such a perfect polity would not look like persons raised under less opportune circumstances. Ideal citizens would differ from others – including Genevans – for example, whom he instructs "you are neither Romans, nor Spartans; you are not even Athenians. Leave aside these great names that do not suit you. You are Merchants, Artisans, Bourgeois ... people for whom every liberty is only a means for acquiring without obstacle and for possessing in safety" (*LEM*, IX, 292–293/881). Genevans' preoccupation with modern liberty reaps material rewards but is ill-suited for achieving either the kind or degree of freedom Rousseau associates with self-governance.

Lastly, a third reason for concluding that Rousseau's laws are drafted by the people alone is that citizens raised under good laws would not need the supervision required of a large majority. It is not only legislative expertise that is superfluous but also policing. He writes that, unlike the citizens of Geneva, "a restless, unoccupied, turbulent people always ready, for lack of private business, to get mixed up in that of the State, needs to be held within bounds" (*LEM*, IX, 293/881). Even in Geneva "the public order of your general Council is the easiest thing in the world; let them sincerely wish to establish it for the public good, then everything will be free there, and everything will take place there more tranquilly than today" (*LEM*, VII, 252/832). This placidity originates from Genevans' differences from Greeks and Romans in the measure of their private pursuits and occupations. One can speculate that subjects in Rousseau's just state would not need "to be held within bounds" because of their education and good citizenship. Although the philosopher bars the people from self-convoking themselves into an assembly because, among other reasons, he fears the risks of "seditious tumult" (*CS*, III:xiii, 111/426; III:xviii, 119/435), he does not appear to consider these risks so great as to bar them from drafting their own laws.

Against this textual evidence it is possible to argue that a number of other passages in Rousseau's political writings reveal agenda-setting by the government to be permissible so long as the people are left free to discuss, modify or oppose initiatives. In my opinion, these passages demonstrate persuasively that the Genevan does not believe the people must draft their own laws inside even the best of states. On the topic of agenda-setting, specifically, across his corpus he asks only that the people's right to propose, discuss and oppose legislation be respected.

Notably, Rousseau labels agenda-setting by government to be one of "the best maxims that good sense could dictate concerning the constitution of a government" (*DI*, 3/111) and he identifies Geneva, where this was the norm, as being the basis for the positive political program of the *Social Contract* expressly. While still condemning its systemic legislative flaws, he writes "I took your Constitution, which I found to be beautiful, as the model for political institutions" and asks, "that primitive Contract, that essence of Sovereignty, that empire of the Laws, that institution of Government ... isn't this stroke for stroke the image of your Republic, since its birth up to this day?" (*LEM*, VI, 233/809).

In his discussion of the "right of legislation" in the *Dédicace*, specifically, he also remarks that "I would have sought a Country" where "everyone did not have the power to propose new Laws according to his fancy; that this right belonged exclusively to the Magistrates" (*DI*, 5/113–114). Pointedly, in this letter the philosopher is not merely describing a status quo situation but positively endorsing ("*J' aurois cherché un Païs*") legislative interference by magistrates. His belief is that a people ought to decide "upon the report of their Chiefs the most important public affairs" (*DI*, 6/114). Why this is so is carefully explained:

> however useful new Laws might be, their advantages are almost always less certain than their dangers are great. In this regard when the Citizen, when the Bourgeois has proposed his opinion he has done his duty, he ought moreover to have enough confidence in his Magistrate to judge him capable of weighing the advantage of what he proposes to him and inclined to approve it if he believes it useful to the public good. Thus the Laws has very wisely provided that the establishment and even the proposing of such innovations would not pass without the approval of the Councils, and that is what the negative right they lay claim to consists of, which, according to me, incontestably belongs to them.
>
> (*LEM, VIII, 264–265/846–847*)

It is in this vein that Rousseau is critical of Geneva's constitution for forbidding the people from exercising legislative oversight but *not* for permitting the government a role in lawmaking. Sovereignty is said to be violated because the *petit Conseil* goes unchecked rather than because this lesser body participates in lawmaking. His complaint is against an inferior body "which alone proposes, which decides first, and whose voice alone, even in its own cause, permits its superiors to have one" (*LEM*, VII, 252/832). The *petit Conseil* "alone has its own activity, that gives theirs to all the others, that in all of them, supporting the resolutions it has taken, gives an opinion two times and votes three times" (*LEM*, VII, 253/832–833). His view is that it is unreasonable "to make it so that none can propose anything" except "those who have the greatest interest in harming it" because "if the existence of the general Council depended completely on the small Council, the general Council would be suppressed forever" (*LEM*, VII, 249/828). In the end, the "sovereign power is enchained" if the people "cannot act except when it pleases your Magistrates, nor speak except when they interrogate" it. (*LEM*, VII, 238/814). If the sovereign cannot act except when permitted by the government than the laws make it "speak as it pleases" since "these Tribunals will certainly not approve propositions that would be prejudicial to them" (*LEM*, VII, 249/827–828). It is apparent that everything is "dead in the Republic" (*LEM*, VII, 252/832) when the sovereign cannot "speak as it pleases," but this is not the same thing as saying that it is only alive when it speaks unassisted.

In this regard, Rousseau's efforts to ensure that the sovereign "speaks as it pleases" can be argued to inform his definition of separation of powers. His barring of any and all forms of legislation by the government (*EP*, 142/244; *CS*, III:i, 166/395; III:iv, 173/404; *LEM*, IV, 232/808) can be demonstrated to refer not to agenda-setting but to impositions placed upon lawmaking that the people cannot overturn. Whenever the majority is prevented from proposing, opposing or deliberating upon a law then it is the government who is sovereign. What divides sovereignty is not the presence of foreigners but the presence of a will that is foreign and binding. Unchecked, government's commands or decrees are wholly illegitimate and yet they can still "pass for expressions of the general will, so long as the Sovereign, being free to oppose them, does not do so" (*CS*, II:I, 145/369), according to Rousseau. It is this express freedom to oppose the chiefs – not the *issuing* of commands personally – that makes rule by government possible.

This interpretation finds precedence in Rousseau's description of the lawgiver in the *Social Contract* as a body that "drafts the laws" and yet has no "legislative right" in the form of a final check (*CS*, II:vii, 156/383). This function, drafting the laws, appears to devolve to the Prince (or government) in Rousseau's comparison between the "mechanic who invents" the laws (the lawgiver) and the "workman" (the Prince) who replaces him. He writes that the Prince "only has to follow the model that the latter should propose. The latter is the mechanic who invents the machine; the former is only the workman who puts it together and starts it running" (*CS*, II:vii, 155/381). In this line the philosopher does not describe the Prince as merely running the system of legislation created by the lawgiver but says that he "puts it together" or assembles it also (*"l'ouvrier qui la monte et la fait marcher"*). Considering that what the lawgiver puts together are laws it is not entirely unreasonable to assume that Rousseau is referring to the assembling of legislation, i.e. that the Prince inherits the lawgiver's power of agenda-setting.

This said, these counter-arguments aside, in my opinion the most convincing of the three textual bases for concluding that it is the people alone who draft the laws (the sovereign proposes the laws unassisted) is the view that experts are superfluous because the general will is universally known. As I note, Rousseau's belief is that when the general will is discernable universally "all the mechanisms of the State are vigorous and simple," and "the common good is clearly apparent everywhere" (*CS*, IV:i, 198/437). With such clarity no citizen would "propose new Laws according to his fancy" (*DI*, 5/114) thus rendering interference by experts an unnecessary risk. Proposals would not be fanciful at all, but "what everyone has already felt" (*CS*, IV:i, 198/437). When this occurs agenda-setting and ratification are nearly seamless acts by the people as they express the general will in unanimity.

In my view, the central problem with this interpretation is that Rousseau characterizes lawmaking in his ideal state as achieving this heightened degree of transparency and yet he simultaneously imposes restrictions upon its exercise. Voting is free and transparent but what takes place before and afterward is decidedly less so. Owing to this difference, the philosopher's comparison between citizens and peasants in Book VI:i of the *Social Contract* can be construed as simply an ideal that the laws ought to embody rather than how this ideal is arrived at in a perfect state. Critically, in this passage Rousseau writes that "to the degree that it becomes necessary to promulgate new [laws], this necessity is universally seen" (*CS*, IV:i, 198/437) and yet nowhere in the political program of the *Social Contract* does he allow the people to freely and regularly convene themselves when this need becomes known. All may recognize the need to pass new laws but the only body authorized to act upon this need on a regular basis is the government (*CS*, III:xiii, 190/426). This is true not only for citizens in states "badly constituted from the beginning" (*CS*, IV:i, 193/437) but also for citizens in states that are well-constituted.

Rousseau's justification for this rule is that the decision to convene must be prescribed by law because it is a particular act. That said, this stricture also appears to derive from his anxiety about the ascent of a "proud and restless" citizenry that, like Rome's unruly *Comitia*, pursues rash or imprudent change. Although his idealized citizens are of a wholly different temperament than the tumultuous or seditious Romans that he (and Montesquieu (1965 [1734], 93)) alternatively praises and condemns, he considers this to be a fragile disposition.[22] He appears to fear the emergence of an inspired

---

[22] On this point see Melzer, *The Natural Goodness of Man*, 172–3.

citizenry that eagerly "rushes" to the assemblies (*CS*, III:xv, 192/429) ever becoming like the ancient Romans; sovereign-members becoming "proud and restless" as the laws weaken over time. Although, he claims that only large states "require supervision [*police*]" and praises Athens' "assembly of several thousands of quick-tempered, ardent, and almost unrestrained Citizens" for needing minimal supervision, he also says that assemblies that number in the thousands or tens of thousands, such as Rome's *Comitia*, require restraint (*CS*, IV:iv, 207/449; *LEM*, VII, 251–252/830–831; IX, 293/881). Like the lawgivers of old, his solution to this problem appears to be a "specific form and formality" for lawmaking that includes, among other things, a role for government in the early stages of the legislative process. Similar to the people's ability to oppose or veto legislative initiatives, however, the philosopher allows the people to self-convene if and when the government fails to exercise its duties in good faith.

Similarly, Rousseau's remarks about the censor reveal a role for government in the early stages of the legislative process. In the *Social Contract*, the censor is said to be an integral part of the state owing to citizens' need for moral rectitude. Unlike the foundational lawgiver, however, the censor is not a transitory body that departs with it but, rather, remains in existence to guide opinion as "legislation weakens" (*CS*, IV:vii, 215/458) as the state needs to be "ceaselessly careful to maintain or revive love of fatherland and good morals among the people" (*EP*, 157/262). The opinions of a people "arise from its constitution," according to Rousseau, and the "Censorship maintains morals by preventing opinions from becoming corrupt; by preserving their rectitude through wise application" of the laws (*CS*, IV:vii, 215/459). For these "wise applications" to be effective, though, it is necessary that the people be kept unaware of the actual intent behind certain laws in order to maintain their desired effect upon opinion. Popular ignorance makes it possible for the censor to enunciate the status of opinion on a particular question through reference to a law that, on its face, appears wholly unrelated. This is why, according to the Genevan, laws designed to influence "morals, customs, and especially opinion" are that "which the great Legislator attends in secret while appearing to limit himself to the particular regulations that are merely the sides of the arch of which morals, slower to arise, form at last the unshakable Keystone" (CS, II:xii, 165/394). This fourth "kind of law" that Rousseau assigns to the censor to apply wisely (CS, IV:vii, 215/459) works best when the true object of each and every regulation is not fully known. All ought to know the intent behind most laws but not *every* law. Notably, in II:xii of the *Social Contract*, Rousseau refers to constitutional legislation, specifically, rather than to the commands or decrees that would fall under government's jurisdiction even before the lawgiver departs. All of these (constitutional law, commands and decrees) are the object of censorship.

Assuming that it were the case that the right of initiation belongs to the people alone then this aspect of Rousseau's theory is an enigma. Drafting all of the laws on their own, the people would be aware of their original intent and – all secrets known – the censor would be left having to search for hidden applications of the law where there were none. Conversely, as the censor declared the status of prevailing opinion on any issue of controversy or recently passed law the people would be able to challenge its judgment as a matter of right. Not only its discretion but also the very basis of this discretion would be in dispute (its chief source of political power). In his *Letters Written from the Mountain*, Rousseau asserts that when there is a controversy over interpretations of the law than, at least in Geneva, the arbiter ought to be the people (the *Conseil général*). It is "up to the equity of the Magistrate to fix their meaning in practice" but "this right does not at all go to the point of changing the literal sense of the laws." When there is a danger of such obfuscation then the "good sense that pronounces is then found in the general Council" (*LEM*, VIII, 277/861). Yet such similar-type good sense in his just state would prove to be highly problematic for laws intended to preserve good *moeurs*. The censor would have to enunciate the status of opinion on a particular question without reference to any law or only to those laws that are drafted by all. Yet a solution to this conundrum exists if it is assumed that the people do not legislate unassisted. What the people enjoy, as Rousseau highlights in the *Letters*, is a non-exclusive right to participate in lawmaking. They may oppose, discuss and initiate legislation but it is assumed that not every law will be decided by the people alone.

It can be argued that each of these arguments gives weight to the notion that agenda-setting is, in many ways, a joint effort between citizens and their appointed elite. Although, it may not always be the case when the state is at its apogee or zenith, it is true that the fundamentals of the two sides of this relationship reveal a role for experts in legislative agenda-setting. As some commentators have remarked, it is the prominence of this function that gives substance to the view that Rousseau surreptitiously devolves political power to an elite in his *patrie*. The Genevan's willingness to accept the presence of experts in such a critical capacity is said to give support to the strong argument for representation even if a state is well-ordered. What happens after the departure of the lawgiver is said to reveal a surprisingly prominent role for agenda-setting experts in the drafting of the laws.

Challenging the veracity of this reading (its over-emphasis in the other direction, by my view) it can be asserted that the sovereignty of the people is protected despite the presence of legislative experts in Rousseau's state. Although, it is the case that experts are free to participate in the drafting of the laws this function is never allowed to supplant or replace the people as the locus of political power. Agenda-setting by experts does not usurp indivisible rule because final decisionmaking power over all aspects of lawmaking resides elsewhere.

DEBUNKING THE STRONG ARGUMENT FOR LEGISLATIVE REPRESENTATION IN ROUSSEAU'S MATURE STATE

In the *Social Contract*, Rousseau describes the lawgiver as a transitional figure who uses the laws to edify *moeurs*, inculcate Roman-style civic virtue, and fosters corporate unity among the citizenry.

The lawgiver voluntarily retires, according to the Genevan, when the citizenry are morally and politically mature enough to legislate the laws by themselves. Although *every* ratified law is an expression of the general will and Rousseau is unambiguous that laws are legitimate for this reason alone, he prescribes this transition believing that citizens will be cognizant of the general will enough to be trusted with both ends of democratic lawmaking. Assuming total control, citizens are empowered to appoint a body from amongst themselves to initiate the laws that the community, as a whole, will ratify in person.

For some commentators this latter act of naming a second body to initiate the laws is of marginal importance, while for others it is evidence of Rousseau's distrust of majority rule. With respect to the former, in the widest sense "popular sovereignty is tenable because the citizens have been 'educated', 'formed' [and] 'guided'."[23] Having "borne the true yoke of laws" (*CS*, II:x, 162/390) citizens in his later state are no longer similar to the ancient Hebrews, "a swarm of unfortunate fugitives" and a "wandering and servile" horde in need of guidance (*CGP*, II, 171–172/956–957). This interpretation emphasizes how a citizenry practically "self-impose" legislation in the strong and intuitively satisfying sense of ratifying *and* initiating the laws that express their will. This notion is consonant with Rousseau's description of this body as agents or *"commissaires"* of the laws, rather than as *"representants,"* to identify this body's bearing as an agent of the sovereign (*CS*, III:xv, 192/429–430).[24]

With respect to the second reading, the view is that Rousseau proposes the appointment of an elite body of aristocrats from among

---

[23] Lester G. Crocker, *Jean Jacques Rousseau: The Prophetic Voice (1758–1778)*, II, New York: Collier-Macmillan, 1973, 182.

[24] In her classic study, Hanna F. Pitkin distinguishes *representants* from *commissaires* as a variable of the latter's subordination to the majority. Pitkin writes that "'commissioner' (unlike 'deputy') suggest[s] that the representative is sent to the central government with explicit instructions, or to do a particular thing ... And it is suggested that those sending him are a unified and official body ... There is no doubt that ... commissioners ... are subordinates of those who send them." Pitkin, *The Concept of Representation*, 134.

the citizenry because he has larger ambitions in mind. The true locus of political power in the republic, this body is responsible for the day-to-day functions of the government as well as the initiating of sovereign laws. Together with enacting decrees, the constitutional laws (*loix fondamentales*) are drafted by representatives and voted upon by the community at large. Voting by citizens is infrequent because the people are narrowly restricted to constitutional lawmaking alone or, as Shklar describes, "not called upon to make or remake laws but to reassert" their "willingness to abide by the contract and to live in justice."[25] The real locus of power in the state, representatives actually do much more: the "genuine statesman" extends "his respectable dominion over wills even more than over actions" (*EP*, 147/250). The "greatest talent of leaders is to disguise their power to make it less odious, and to manage the state so peacefully that it seems to have no need for managers" (*EP*, 147/250). More pointedly,

> If it is good to know how to use men as they are, it is better still to make them what one needs them to be ... it is certain that people are in the long run what the government makes them. Warriors, citizens, men when it wishes; mob and rabble when it so pleases. And every prince who scorns his subjects dishonors himself by showing that he did not know how to make them worthy of esteem. Form men, therefore, if you want to command men. If you want the laws to be obeyed, make them beloved, so that for men to do what they should, they need only think they ought to do it.
>
> (*EP*, 148/251–252)

Similarly, in the *Social Contract*, Rousseau advises political leaders to "reform men's opinions and their morals will purify themselves" for "one always likes what is beautiful" but "it is this judgment that may be mistaken. Therefore, the problem is to regulate this judgment" (*CS*, IV:vii, 215/458). More so than anywhere else, he

---

[25] Shklar, *Men and Citizens*, 181.

appears to adhere to these words the most fully in *Poland*. For example, Julia Simon-Ingram writes that Poles "believe that they freely pursue their interests in an independent and democratic nation. In point of fact, their interests – the public interest – have been determined for them by Rousseau/the Legislator."[26] Through emotional oratory, sensual illustration, colorful examples, etc., the lawgiver fixes the "pleasures, desires and tastes" and condition the people to reject alternatives to its proposals. All are "brainwashed" to vote for the general will and nothing else.

In a unique feature of Rousseau's system, this level of interference by those who draft the laws is not said to divide sovereignty. According to the philosopher, agenda-setting by experts in a state that is justly ordered does not constitute representation, alienation, or a division of the general will in any way. This corporate will, made explicit only at the very moment of the ratifying vote, is entirely vested in the majority and its integrity is preserved by the absence of *commissaires* during the final vote. In the *Social Contract* it is this consistency that makes possible (and plausible) the strong argument for representation. Formally, at least, an elected elite can do most of the legislating in his state and the philosopher can still claim with consistency that *"la Souveraineté ne peut étre réprésentée"* (*CS*, III:xv, 192/429).

As congruous as the strong argument for representation is with Rousseau's unique definition of sovereignty (which I do not deny), it is also problematic on a number of levels that this congruousness veils. In this regard, Rousseau may not be a staunch democrat but he is also not an orthodox republican. Of these difficulties, the most conspicuous, arguably, is the obvious incompatibility of the strong argument for representation with the philosopher's frequent and vociferous protests against representation. One can argue that Rousseau expresses these protests repeatedly and forcefully enough to, at the very least, earn himself the benefit of the doubt that his intent really *is* to prevent representatives from encroaching upon the

---

[26] Julia Simon-Ingram, "Rousseau and the Problem of Community: Nationalism, Civic Virtue, Totalitarianism," *History of European Ideas*, 16 (1–3) 1993: 27, 39.

legislative power of the majority. This can be witnessed in the *Social Contract* as he asserts that "sovereignty ... consists essentially in the general will, and the will cannot be represented. Either it is itself or it is something else; there is no middle ground" (*CS*, III:xv, 192/429–430). This "middle ground" appears to be not a purely theoretical space arising from the philosopher's idiosyncratic view of sovereignty, but something more concrete resulting from his knowledge of how political power is actually exercised and his fears about how it is expanded. This is also evident in his warning in the *Social Contract* not to let the polity grow large enough that "the leaders, dispersed to govern it, can each make decisions for the Sovereign" (*CS*, III:v, 175/407). Although the leaders may be endowed with "probity, enlightenment [and] experience" it is the people whom, as I mention earlier, are "the voice of God." He laments elsewhere that "this sacred voice is always weak in affairs against the outcry of power, and the complaint of oppressed innocence is uttered in murmurs despised by tyranny" (*LEM*, VIII, 278/862).

More generally, it can be asserted that unlike the constitutional democracies in existence in contemporary Europe, there is no legislative separation or balance of powers anywhere in Rousseau's sovereignty in the sense that either of these terms (separation and balancing) mean within the parlance of modern constitutionalism. Rousseau believes in separating or balancing the powers *within* the executive and lauds the *gouvernement mixte* of the English constitution, but nowhere in his writings does he propose a constitutional separating or balancing in the traditional sense of dividing or sharing sovereignty in order to *restrain* it. Only acts of government can be restrained, never sovereignty (Cobban, 1934, 82). In his mature state, Rousseau empowers an elected elite to shape the constitutional laws but he stops short of authorizing this body to serve as a final check. Instead, a single and undivided majority is the final arbiter over every law put before it and those laws not put before it, such as decrees, can be overturned by an overhaul of the government, if necessary.

Within a purely legislative context, this hybrid cameralist arrangement is different from both the ancient mixed constitution and our modern understanding of separation of powers in which the "powers belonging to one of the departments" ought not possess "an overruling influence over the others."[27] With regard to the former, Rousseau does not construe representatives who propose the laws to be "balancing" the majority who ratify them in the same way, for example, that Aristotle believes that oligarchs ought to balance democrats' extreme view of justice and vice versa through a rotation of political offices (*Politics*, III:9) or a collegial-style power-sharing arrangement. As his description of the Roman republic's constitution in the *Social Contract* illustrates, such divisions can exist within the government but not within the sovereign.

The philosopher does describe the Roman senators as temporarily holding "in check a proud and restless people" (*CS*, IV:iv, 207/449) and praises "a wisely tempered Tribunate" for being "the firmest support of a good constitution" (*CS*, IV:v, 211/454), but neither of these bodies in any way "balances" the majority by intermittently substituting their own will for that of the Comitia's or *restraining* the will of the majority by way of a final check. Rather, the will of one faction is *entirely* and *permanently* subject to the will of its opposite at the point of ratification. The will of the majority overrides and trumps the wills of everybody else – including that of the wise elite responsible for initiating the laws. For Aristotle, this would be tantamount to compelling oligarchs to govern according to a democratic principle of justice that gives equal weight to the many in the final outcome of legislation.

This idea, inconsistent with Nadia Urbinati's description of Rousseau's polity as a "delegated democracy," challenges the notion that magistrates are endowed with the power to "overrule the sovereign" and may "disobey the will of the people" without the fear of popular supervision. It is untrue that "delegated power plays the

---

[27] James Madison, Alexander Hamilton and John Jay, *The Federalist*, Philadelphia: The Franklin Library, 1977 [1788], No. 48:2, 355.

greatest role in the life of the state and is kept out of citizens' sight and control" and that magistrates only speciously "lack the formal power to make decisions in the sovereign's place."[28] Rather, it is the people who must always give the last word and it is they alone who make their wants binding by way of the laws. According to Rousseau, "the *dominant* will of the prince is not or should not be anything except the general will or the law ... As soon as he wants to derive from himself some *absolute* or independent act, the bond tying the whole begins to loosen" (*CS*, III:i, 169/399; my italics). There should never be any ambiguity about who controls this public force for "the general will that should direct the State is not that of a past time but of the present moment, and the true characteristic of sovereignty is that there is always agreement on ... the direction of the general will and the use of public force" (*MG*, I:iv, 88/296). Such a need for agreement is ancillary to the prior question of who "should direct the State" or the absolute decisionmaking power of the people.

More broadly, this limited argument for "delegated democracy" can be called into question by a number of statements that the philosopher makes in the *Social Contract* and *Considerations on the Government of Poland* that assign a wide range of legislative control downward. Rousseau writes, for example, that "if the Sovereign wants to govern, or if the magistrate wants to make laws" the result is that "disorder replaces rule" (*CS*, III:xv, 192/430; III:I, 167/397). This passage might be read as referring to the constitutional laws exclusively, but this view appears to be somewhat skewed in light of his other comment that "the government receives from the Sovereign the *orders* that it gives to the people" (*CS*, III:i, 167/396; my italics). Elsewhere, he also emphasizes how laws passed by the sovereign, on occasion, can "punish" [*punissent*] subjects. For each citizen "consents to all the laws" and even "to those that punish him when he dares to violate one of them" (*CS*, IV: ii, 200/440). Such an outcome

---

[28] Nadia Urbinati, *Representative Democracy: Principles and Genealogy*, Chicago and London: The University of Chicago Press, 2006, 77, 85.

is inconsistent with a highly liberal interpretation of constitutional lawmaking in his state that would, by definition, still be limited to articulating the terms for those acts of ordinary legislation that do punish citizens.

Similarly, the models and ancient examples that Rousseau cites from Rome, Sparta and Athens illustrate a heightened level of popular participation in politics that is far beyond what would be necessary or possible if the people were restricted to constitutional lawmaking alone. It is his view that in a well-ordered polity the people would be politically concerned enough with "public affairs" to want to "rush" to the assemblies (CS, III:xv, 192/429). Asking readers to "let us consider what can be done on the basis of what has been done," he recounts that the Greeks were "constantly assembled at the public square" and rarely "a few weeks went by" when Rome's four hundred thousand citizens "was not assembled" (CS, III:xii, 189/425; III;xv, 193/430).

In line with these observations about Greece and Rome, the philosopher's own constitution for Poland proposes instructions for a wide array of functions within the Diet that would ordinarily fall under the jurisdiction of the government if the sovereign were restricted to constitutional lawmaking alone. He proposes, for example, that "the Deputies' instructions must be drawn up with great care, with regard to both the items announced on the agenda and the other needs present in the State or in the Province" (CGP, VII, 190/979). Transferring agenda-setting power away from the Diet to the people, Rousseau is explicit that it is not simply those laws pertaining to the structure or reform of Poland's constitution that the people are to adjudicate over but, rather, also the various "items announced on the agenda" of the Diet's mandate. Though this list is to be drawn up by a commission presided over by the Marshal of the Dietine, deputies are compelled to render "a strict account to their constituents of their conduct at the Diet" (CGP, VII, 190–191/979–980). Rousseau is emphatic that each deputy do "nothing contrary to the express will of his constituents" for

with each word that the Deputy says at the Diet, with each step
he takes, he must see himself in advance under the eyes of his
constituents, and feel the influence that their judgment will
have both over his plans for advancement and over the esteem of
his compatriots ... for in the end the Nation sends Deputies to
the Diet, not in order to state their private sentiment there, but
in order to declare the wills of the Nation.

(*CGP*, VII, 190/980)

Whichever is the accurate (or *most* accurate) understanding of
the sovereign's proper legislative domain, it can be asserted that the
belief by Shklar and others that constitutional lawmaking results in
an "immobile democracy" can still be faulted. For example, Rousseau
asserts in all of his political writings that it is passivity, more than
anything else, that is the death knell to the body politic (*CS*, III:xv
passim) and he proposes that citizens be actively engaged in lawmaking to avoid exactly the kinds of dangers that befell the British people under parliamentary rule (*CS*, III:xv, 192/430). Likewise, he does
not believe that a stipulation of proportional majority rule would
serve as any kind of a de facto entrenchment clause inside of a well-
ordered state. This is because such a stipulation would be immaterial if most voters are nearly unanimous inside of a just state.[29] Only
a very divided people who reside in a very fractious state ought to be
forced to live under entrenched laws.

Elaborating upon the need for robust political engagement to
achieve such high numbers, in a persuasive essay, Stephen G. Affeldt
describes Rousseauian lawmaking as an expression of "continuous
willing" or "continuous contracting" by the sovereign that precludes
any kind of a "settled" or established body of laws. The sovereign's
role, among other things, is to "force men to be free" by compelling
them continuously to will together a general will so that "genuine

[29] I am grateful to a student of mine, Bjorn Gomes Wee, for pointing out to me how
this frequent criticism concerning proportional majority voting in the *Social
Contract* is only intended to entrench laws in polities that are a distant departure from Rousseau's ideal.

society among them" can exist.[30] The Genevan's command that "whoever refuses to obey the general will shall be constrained to do so by the entire body" (CS, I:vii, 141/364) is, according to Affeldt, meant to be taken literally and requires individual sovereign-members to constrain others "to turn against the private will and toward participation in the continuous constitution of a general will."[31] More than any kind of coercive strictures, forcing men to be free entails day-to-day "philosophical instruction, critique, and self-presentation" by sovereign-members to attract others to "the currently unrealized state of ourselves."[32]

From Rousseau's constitution for Poland and his proposals for the *Social Contract*, it is possible to speculate about what the legislative functions of the sovereign *would actually be* beyond will formation. Although the philosopher is parsimonious in his discussion of the minutiae of sovereign rule, his suggestions for reforming the Diet in *Considerations on the Government of Poland* make possible some speculation in this direction. As he describes, the sole function of the sovereign assembly is lawmaking and any activity that is extraneous to this end is beyond its jurisdiction. This said, the single criterion that he uses to define a law – a generality of object and source – confers upon the assembly a broad authority to pass legislation that affects all of the people directly.

According to Rousseau, the assembly can "designate the qualities" that entitle membership to "Classes of Citizens" (CS, II:vi, 153/379) so it could, presumably, pass a graduated tax code that specifies the earnings that entitle membership to different economic classes of citizens. Similarly, it could decide the general criteria to be used to draw up a slate of candidates before an election or determine the criteria that would decide how funds would be allocated in the state's annual budget (even if it could not draft the figures for the budget itself). Presumably,

---

[30] Stephen G. Affeldt, "The Force of Freedom: Rousseau on Forcing to be Free," *Political Theory* 27 (3) 1999: 306.
[31] Affeldt, "The Force of Freedom," 314.
[32] Affeldt, "The Force of Freedom," 318, 323.

the legislative assembly could also draw up a criminal code that, in exacting detail, specifies the "qualities determining who has a right" to greater or lesser penalties for different classes of crimes. Requiring "a plurality" for "matters of simple administration" or "other routine and momentary business," "three-quarters of the suffrages" for more significant legislation, and "two thirds in matters of State" (CGP, IX, 204/997), the assembly's level of activity would be a variable of the importance of the issues before it and the level of activity by government that the assembly might need to counter (CS, III:xiii, 190/426; CGP, VII, 186/975). With respect to the latter, if the government is strong the assembly could meet frequently for terms of no more than six weeks which, according to the philosopher, would be "sufficient for the ordinary needs of the State" (CGP, VII, 191/981). Presumably, the terms for constitutional or other types of extraordinary legislation could last much longer. The assembly could also decide in a very general fashion, perhaps, "the items announced on the agenda" in the same manner that Rousseau prescribes Poles be permitted to instruct and decide the agenda of the Diet (CGP, VII, 190/979).[33]

Whether or not this somewhat speculative view of the sovereign is overstated, what is accurate is that the majority in Rousseau's state is neither overtly nor surreptitiously reduced to inertia by having its role diminished to an exclusively acclamatory body. More meaningful than what the sovereign actually *does* is the influence that it *wields* by way of the institutional checks that are obligatory. At no moment in the lawmaking process do representatives substitute their will for that of the sovereign's or restrain its will for any elongated period of time.

---

[33] This interpretation is consistent with Montesquieu's view of legislative mandates. According to Montesquieu, it is unnecessary that the people legislate personally so long as their influence upon the laws is expressed generally. He believes that it is "not necessary that the representatives, who have been generally instructed by those who have chosen them, be instructed about each matter of business in particular, as is the practice in the Diets of Germany." Montesquieu, *The Spirit of the Laws*, trans. and ed. Anne Cohler, Basia Miller and Harold Stone, Cambridge and London: Cambridge University Press, 1989 [1748], II:vi, 159.

Unlike Sparta's "static constitution by autonomasia" that Sartori describes Rousseau taking as his model,[34] the lawmaking process and overall political program of the *Social Contract* are designed to ward off passivity, inertia and autonomasia in any form. And none of the proposals above, although undeniably cumbersome, is by itself incredible enough to dismiss outright. One can argue that sometimes it really is the case that citizens will want to "rush" to the assemblies to "maintain the social treaty" (*CS*, III:xv, 192/429). As the frequent mass political rallies that have taken place in various Eastern and Western European cities over the past two decades over such controversial issues as democratization, arms control, globalization and immigration illustrate, this is what actually occurs. The continuous appeal of such issues to garner mass support demonstrates, at least theoretically, the possibility of citizens remaining intimately engaged with and by public issues over long periods of time.

Considering everything said above, it is significant that Rousseau does choose, in the end, to allow for the subdivision of legislative power between representatives and the majority in a non-traditional way in the *Social Contract*. He permits a form of separation of powers that gives voice to the few among the many most adroit at framing the general will. The flipside of the argument above asks "What is the legislative role of representatives in Rousseau's mature state?"

ROUSSEAU'S OTHER CRITICISM OF DEMOCRACY: A SINGLE BODY THAT INITIATES AND RATIFIES THE LAWS

As I discuss above, Rousseau's reasoning behind his retiring of the foundational lawgiver in the *Social Contract* is not entirely self-evident. Considering that every ratified law is an expression of the general will and that this corporate will remains legitimate before

---

[34] Sartori, *The Theory of Democracy Revisited*, II, 331n.

and after the lawgiver departs, the rationale for transferring agenda-setting authority to the people is somewhat curious. Why not simply choose another lawgiver?

The first section of this chapter attempted to answer this question by showing, in part, that it is the philosopher's intent that the legislative role played by *commissaires* is different from the lawgiver who, like Moses, is confronted with a "wandering and servile" horde or, like Lycurgus, encountered a "people degraded by servitude" (*CGP*, II, 172/956–957). The question that Rousseau sets out in Book II:vi of the *Social Contract*, "How will a blind multitude, which often does not know what it wants because it rarely knows what is good for it, execute by itself an undertaking as vast and as difficult as a system of legislation?" is *not* the problem to be solved by *commissaires* in his later state. By the time the lawgiver departs to his "future glory" in "the passage of time" (*CS*, II:vii, 154/381) it is no longer the case that the people have "not yet borne the true yoke of laws" (*CS*, II:x, 162/390). Rather, a cohesive legislative system has long been in force and what is necessary now is for *commissaires* merely to "follow the model that the other should propose" and keep the "machine" "running" in order to save the sovereign from inadvertently undermining the body of laws erected by the lawgiver (*CS*, II:vii, 154–155/381).

Unlike "the complex process of remaking the individual, the Legislator's principal task,"[35] *commissaires* of the laws are responsible for maintaining the legislative machine (to stay with Rousseau's metaphor) that guides and upholds the sovereign will. Ideally, this will has already "reached its highest possible point of perfection" (*CS*, II:vii, 155/381) and is self-reinforcing owing to the procedural incentives within the lawmaking process.[36] For this reason, *commissaires*

---

[35] Crocker, *Jean Jacques Rousseau*, 181.

[36] Anticipating Tocqueville's praise of juries, Rousseau considers self-governance to be a politically educative mechanism for fostering corporate unity and civic virtue. The *Social Contract's* principle of equity compels each to consider all when considering his or her own interests in a manner that engenders civic

need not *remake* individuals or feel themselves "capable of changing human nature" but, rather, "extend and strengthen" (*E*, I, 39/248) their natural dispositions to give their passions "order and regularity" (*E*, IV, 219/500) by way of initiatives conducive to "wise applications" (*CS*, IV:vii, 215/459) of the laws. Such an elite is composed not of extraordinary figures from without – such as the foundational lawgiver – but of fellow citizens from within who display "probity, enlightenment [and] experience" (*CS*, III:v, 175/408), among other virtues that are potentially within reach of all community members.

Critically, this expert body's criteria for selection differs radically from both the ancient democratic and the modern republican criteria used to judge legislators' qualifications in the past. Seeking to avoid any kind of pure identification between the people and *commissaires*, Rousseau rejects any Athenian-style reliance upon lot, sortition, or any other random method of selection designed to produce "descriptive representation." A perfect "correspondence ... resemblance and reflection" between electors and elected with the latter "standing for"[37] the people is not his goal. Conversely, unlike the franchise restrictions in use in Whig England or in the United States before 1846, Rousseau rejects any constraints upon the franchise that might facilitate the election of elites whose notable

responsibility. Any psychological "conditioning," so to speak, is unnecessary because the procedures that accompany self-governance serve to *self-condition* citizens to pass good laws. This self-conditioning is not permanent but it is less perilous than surreptitiously delegating political power to executives serving as an elected proxy for the lawgiver.

[37] Pitkin, *The Concept of Representation*, 61; considering the origin of this type of "standing for" or descriptive representation, Pitkin writes that "the etymological development in this period is confused, and the available evidence is not conclusive, but it suggests" that at this time "terms like 'represent' were first applied to the Parliament as an image of the whole nation" and that Hobbes was one of the first to use the terms "represent" and "Representative" in this larger sense. On whether Hobbes was "making a brilliant application, or merely expressing what was the current conception of the terms," Pitkin is uncertain, but "the earliest application I have come across of the noun 'representative' to a member of Parliament occurs in 1651" and that "it is also the year in which Hobbes published the *Leviathan*, in the midst of this etymological development." See *The Concept of Representation*, 250.

qualitative differences of wealth, status, privilege, rank, etc., would distinguish them from the general character of the people. Instead, he proposes something closer to the original natural aristocracy that he dismisses as appropriate only to simple peoples (CS, III:v, 174–175/406).[38]

In the *Social Contract*, he argues that the best system is one where the whole of the people elect only those endowed with qualities natural to all. Lauding Rome, where "no law received sanction, no magistrate was elected except in the Comitia" (CS, IV:iv, 207/449)[39] Rousseau believes that those elected should be chosen for their "probity, enlightenment [and] experience" solely (CS, III:v, 175/408). The wealthy have more time to participate in politics but "personal merit offers more important reasons for preference than does riches" (CS, III:v, 176/408). Calling it "aristocracy properly so-called," his ideal *commissaires* are aristocratic only in the sense that they are endowed with a larger *degree* of natural qualities common to all.

Requiring that the government as a whole be chosen from among the people, the use of elections capitalizes upon the natural differences among men but – critically – not any differences resulting from wealth, privilege, title, status or any other social basis. This emphasis upon the differences in degree of citizens' natural attributes is a source of commonality between the government and the sovereign that is designed to guarantee that those delegates who draft laws do not do so according to an alien will. Natural differences should not pose a risk to liberty because "our natural passions" are "the instruments of our freedom; they tend to preserve us. All those which subject us and destroy us come from elsewhere" (E, 212/491).

This view of *commissaires* is different from Rousseau's description of the lawgiver as a being who "saw all of men's passions yet experienced none of them; who had no relationship at all to our nature yet knew it thoroughly" (CS, II:vii, 154/381). The elite who

---

[38] Gildin, *Rousseau's Social Contract*, 107–108, 110.
[39] See Gildin, *Rousseau's Social Contract*, 110.

inherits the office of this extraordinary being do "experience" passion and are of "our nature" because they are chosen by and among
the people for attributes common to all. Assuming that the vote is
also free, this combination of checks allows for the benefits of legislative expertise while ensuring that popular participation in lawmaking is not reduced to acclamation.

RESOLVING THE TENSION BETWEEN AGENDA-SETTING
AND MAJORITY RULE

This chapter has sought to illuminate an underexamined aspect of
Rousseau's political theory: the complexities associated with legislative initiation in his mature state. In explaining these complexities, I have attempted to show how one of the earliest and most
original theorists of participatory democracy strove to reconcile the
tension between democracy's dual needs of agenda-setting expertise
and majority rule. I demonstrated that, unlike twentieth-century
theorists such as Benjamin R. Barber, Rousseau believes that legislative experts can serve a vital function within a strong democracy
if appropriately checked. These constraints include, among other
things, persuasive disincentives to prevent any "manufacturing"
of popular consent by a legislative elite. Ideally, in a participatory
democracy expert agenda-setters would enhance and facilitate citizen participation rather than foster passivity or, worse yet, "immo-
bility" among the majority. Toward this end, *commissaires* or, more
conventionally, representatives do play a role in Rousseau's bifur-
cated legislative system but one that is functionally dissimilar to
that of the foundational lawgiver. More important than outside
guidance by experts are the politically educative and self-reinforcing
benefits of democratic participation. For this and other reasons, few
recent interpretations are more at odds with the word and the spirit
of the *Social Contract* than those that elevate representatives into
the locus of political power.

3 Democracy and vote rigging

In the *Social Contract* the most politically significant activity of the people is the ratifying of the laws. Unlike representative systems of government in which power is shared between citizens and their chosen delegates or allotted to the latter with periodic checks, the final arbiter of the laws is always the people in a well-ordered state. It is the people alone who legislate all of the constitutional laws and it is they who, by way of the institutional restraints that I describe in Chapter 6, exercise implicit control over executive decrees. If a measure is enacted that proves to be unpopular a citizenry may replace the government or any future regime that allows such measures to remain in force, by right. Although such an outcome ought to be unlikely it is not forbidden or made to be so cumbersome as to be impossible, even with a proportional majority. Rousseau proposes a relatively high threshold for the vote not because he seeks to empower a chosen elite surreptitiously but, rather, to avoid any need to disempower a chosen elite overtly or covertly. Stable laws require stable majorities.

As discussed earlier, the process of ratifying the laws begins with their formal drafting. Similar to statecraft in the ancient world, at the foundation of Rousseau's state this vital function is the duty of the lawgiver and afterward it falls upon the shoulders of the people and to those experts from whom they seek assistance. Prior to this momentous transition though, the lawgiver's role is to initiate laws that accurately mirror the general will while simultaneously strengthening *moeurs* to prepare the people for self-legislation. Afterwards, it is the citizenry alone that must undertake the first of these tasks with the second charge falling to administrators or magistrates. Assuming that the lawgiver has been effective at its job of transforming disparate individuals into a "part of a larger whole" (*CS*, II:vii, 155/381) then unmediated lawmaking ought to be achievable because *moeurs* and the laws are in harmony with the general will.

Although the heavy-lifting of sovereign rule might be said to be the psychological transformation of the people into a homogeneous corporate unit it should be emphasized that voting, specifically, is instrumental to this transformation because it is a procedural act designed to produce "an admirable agreement between interest and justice" (*CS*, II:iv, 149/374). In his political writings, repeatedly, Rousseau emphasizes that voting is pivotal to make individuals sensitive to larger public demands by giving "common deliberations a quality of equity."

Toward this end, citizens' awareness of the laws' generality compels each individual to consider his fellows and their status relative to his own in a way that he would not do otherwise. According to the philosopher, this identification should be considered free because the procedures for realizing justice, unlike the strictures to promote the unity of the sovereign will, do not require any direction by the lawgiver to succeed. All that is required is corporate unity and voting is free to the extent that it is proceduralized in his later state. When the philosopher speaks of the "free vote of the people" (*CS*, II:vii, 156/383) in the *Social Contract* it is not owing to error or duplicity but because "interest and justice" acquire common ground procedurally. The "free vote of the people" refers to the transparency of this process inside of the assembly, expressly.

In the *Social Contract* each citizen is compelled by the procedures that underpin voting to harmonize his interests with others in a way that creates what John Rawls terms a "sense of justice." As all are aware, this confluence is not an aggregation of competing interests or even their unconscious reconciliation but, rather, what all consciously believe to be the preferences of the entire community. Ideally, every citizen ought to be able to make this assessment accurately if there is truly an "admirable agreement" between interest and justice. Each person's vote is the expression of a will that is private only in the sense of being one's own judgment concerning a group preference. When each citizen votes he does so knowing that he will be personally affected by the outcome of his vote but also knowing that his decisions will impact upon the lives of his neighbors. Critically, it is this latter sensitivity to others that distinguishes mere group preferences (*la tout-de-volonté*) from those that can be said to be indicative of the common good (*la volonté générale*). Citizens vote for themselves and for others as a private act of public willing.

Of the publicity of this act, according to some readers the general will is the product of Gramscian-like psychological mediation by the lawgiver and the public censor. F.M. Barnard comments that "opinions concerning a common judgment" are "the work of mediating judgment, without which they might never have come into being" inside of a just state.[1] In a similar vein, Melzer remarks that Rousseau's "solution, in short, is to use fraud, to win over the people's consent through religious deceit."[2] More recently, Bonnie

---

[1] F.M. Barnard, *Self-Direction and Political Legitimacy: Rousseau and Herder*, Oxford: Clarendon Press, 1988, 34–35. Also see Steven Johnston, *Encountering Tragedy: Rousseau and the Project of Democratic Order*, Ithaca: Cornell University Press, 1999, 87; Julia Simon-Ingram, "Rousseau and the Problem of Community: Nationalism, Civic Virtue, Totalitarianism," *History of European Ideas*, 16 (1–3) 1993: 27, 39; Lester G. Crocker, *Rousseau's Social Contract: An Interpretive Essay*, Cleveland: Case Western University Press, 1968, 19, 22; J.L. Talmon, *The Origins of Totalitarian Democracy*, New York: Praeger, 1960; J.W. Chapman, *Rousseau, Totalitarian or Liberal?* New York: Columbia University Press, 1956.

[2] A.M. Melzer, *The Natural Goodness of Man: On the System of Rousseau's Thought*, Chicago: The University of Chicago Press, 1990, 235. While acknowledging "manipulation" on the part of the lawgiver, Melzer also emphasizes the strong juridical elements that underpin the philosopher's "principles of political right" to give substance to popular sovereignty. "In his formal 'principles of political right'" Rousseau "wholly expels the consideration of wisdom and builds the state on the exclusive basis of consent or popular sovereignty, in order to give the state the most unchallengeable juridical structure, to give it the strongest psychological foundation, and to free men from every experience or overt relation of personal dependence; but on the 'other side,' particularly his 'maxims of politics,' he arranges for the secret return of wisdom – its indirect rule through the unofficial, manipulative role of the legislator and of the 'active executive.'" Melzer, *The Natural Goodness of Man*, 244.

Honig, who rejects this view, notes that Rousseau appears to enable "the people's self-governance by compromising their autonomy." His "general will seems to move from being the purely procedural outcome of a political process to being, instead, an extraprocedural outcome by which to judge the products" of an imperfect system.[3] As an enduring criticism, engineering by the lawgiver is said to be what is most significant. Without intensive interference by this body it is believed that the collective deliberations of the sovereign always arrive at a particular outcome and that the activity of self-imposing the laws is of secondary consequence to outside mediation. Political liberty is said to be self-imposed formally, but not substantively, as it is the lawgiver rather than the people that is the true locus of justice inside of a legitimate state. It may be true that liberty demands that the people be "always questioned" by voting but it is even more true that such questioning is moot unless one can be "sure that it is always questioned and that it always answers" (*CS*, IV:I, 199/438). Similar to traditional democracies, it is this activity of *answering* by the people that is most vulnerable to manipulation by extraneous forces.

The textual basis for this longstanding criticism finds substance in *Political Economy*, the *Social Contract* and, to a lesser extent, Rousseau's *Reveries of the Solitary Walker*. It is in these writings that the Genevan highlights the benefits of cunning and deception to effective statecraft and, in the earliest of these three works, praises the use of deception so long as it is consistent with what he terms "the cloak of truth." Reminiscent of his Renaissance Florentine hero, he explains that "the greatest talent of leaders is to disguise their power to make it less odious, and to manage the state so peacefully that it seems to have no need for managers" (*EP*, 147/250). Elaborating on the political usefulness of this public veil he emphasizes in *Political Economy* that it is best to make men into

---

[3] Bonnie Honig, "Between Decision and Deliberation: Political Paradox in Democratic Theory," *American Political Science Review*, 101 (1) February 2007: 4, 5.

"what one needs them to be" and that the "people are in the long run what the government makes them" (*EP*, 148/251–252).

Similarly, Rousseau explains in the *Reveries* that the "purpose" of "allegories or fables" is "to wrap useful truths in easily perceived and pleasing forms" (*RPS*, IV, 32/1029). Analogous to Plato's myth of the metals in the *Republic*, he characterizes such manipulation in his compact as being unproblematic so long as a "de facto lie" is never permitted to betray an essential truth. Asking how "a blind multitude" may execute "by itself an undertaking as vast and as difficult as a system of legislation?" he answers that such a sightless polyglot "must be taught to know what it wants" by, among other things, "altering man's constitution" (*CS*, II:vi, 154/380). To accomplish this formidable task a foundational leader ought to feel no gumption about appealing to "the intervention of heaven" or placing words into "the mouths of the immortals in order to win by divine authority those who cannot be moved by human prudence." Exploiting his genius to "be believed when he declares himself their interpreter," such a leader's aim ought to be to help the people "bear with docility the yoke of public felicity" (*CS*, II: vi, 156–157/383–384).

Of this docility by cunning, one scholar writes that "without thought control, there is no way of achieving complete dependence." What Rousseau really seeks is "the illusion of voluntary commitment."[4] It is the hidden character of such control, specifically, according to John Hope Mason, that "inevitably brings to mind ideas of manipulation, conditioning or, in a chilling phrase our century has invented, *brainwashing*."[5]

POPULAR SOVEREIGNTY AND EXTERNAL "CONDITIONING"

Can the popular vote be socially and politically *engineered* to arrive at a knowable, predictable outcome? Is such interference the

[4] Crocker, *Rousseau's Social Contract: An Interpretive Essay*, 19, 22.
[5] John Hope Mason, "Individuals in Society: Rousseau's Republican Vision," *History of Political Thought*, X (1) spring 1989: 109.

surreptitious onus of liberty in the *Social Contract*? Arguably, the answer to both of these questions turns on the philosopher's arguments concerning the perimeters of the lawgiver's sway over the popular vote. More expressly, it can be said to turn on Rousseau's perception of this body's proper legislative function within a just state. With respect to each of these queries it is possible to demonstrate that the Genevan's Solonic founding father actively participates in will-formation but *not* at a level that undermines "the free vote of the people" to a degree that is decisive. Whatever "will-formation" does exist in Rousseau's legitimate state can be said to be too uncertain to determine or decide the outcome of the vote predictably. Owing to this uncertainty the domain of this institution, for the most part, is heavily circumscribed and limited to engendering a corporate identity among the people exclusively. Unlike Soviet or Maoist-style indoctrination, for example, it can be asserted that there is no hegemonic psychological conditioning in the sense of any doctrinal manipulation of the vote to achieve a predetermined outcome in Rousseau's state. Beyond the creating of an entrenched social and political identity there is no effort to secure any distinctive *content* to the body of the laws. Ideally, a citizenry ought to vote for the lawgiver's initiatives in perfect unanimity but beyond achieving corporate unity this institution's function ceases. It is owing to the limited nature of this role, specifically, that it is credible for Rousseau to describe the laws as originating from a vote that is free.

At the outset, it should be emphasized that *any* interference at all by such an institution should be considered anti-democratic. This intentional curtailing of democracy to objectify the general will inside of a just state can be said to result in a "paradox of politics," as Honig describes, to the extent that "at the moment of founding, no member of the community can yet be said to possess the needed perspective" to "form the rules" to exercise popular sovereignty. This problem is paradoxical because "whatever problems of founding or willing are solved by way of the lawgiver's agency amount to little by comparison with the problems caused thereby for a would-be democracy."[6] Arguably, anticipating this paradox, it can be asserted that the Genevan's emphasis upon unanimity reveals how the most seemingly anti-democratic of his prescriptions do not usurp the autonomy of the popular vote as the lawgiver's "art" is mostly to remove any "tangled and contradictory interests." Toward this end, it is this institution's role to make "clearly apparent" the singular identity that the people are unable to see by themselves at their origin. Altering "man's constitution in order to strengthen it," the lawgiver's function is to ensure that willing itself is reconstituted such that each "can do nothing, except with all the others" (*CS*, II:vii, 155/381–382).

Of this dependency, it seeks a "complete cooperation of the parts" and "the greatest force of the whole" or, in a further echo of Plato, a rallying around the notion that *the whole is good, or Everything is good for the whole* (*letter to Voltaire*, 115/1068). Claiming that "by itself, the people always wants the good, but by itself it does not always see it" (*CS*, II:vii, 154/380) the good to which the philosopher refers is one that is only discernable when the people's "partial and moral existence" is so deeply felt that all atomistic preferences disappear. It is in this Platonic sense that the lawgiver can be said to help the people to perceive the general will but, critically, not predecide the corporeal expression of this perception as a matter of law. Unlike Plato's Republic, justice in Rousseau's state is not an immutable or unchanging standard of justice across time but, rather, mutable to the extent that the vote of the people can go in any direction legitimately and unanimously.

According to the Genevan, the "discovery of the best rules of society," "public enlightenment" and the "union of understanding and will" (*CS*, II:vii, 154/380–381) are realizable ends for persons who believe that *the whole is good.* To facilitate such an extreme identification each citizen need not be manipulated but, rather,

⁶ Honig, "Between Decision and Deliberation," 5, 6.

taught "to appreciate the healthy maxims of politics, and follow the fundamental rules of statecraft." Each must be given the skills "to *weigh* the attraction of present, tangible advantages against the danger of remote, hidden ills" (*CS*, II:vii, 154/380; my italics) and be made to be able to perceive "the advantages he should obtain from the continual deprivations imposed by good laws" (*CS*, II:vii, 156/383). Toward these ends, Rousseau emphasizes the importance of civic education to the goal of making all believe that "everything is good for the whole" in the sense of individuals only considering "their persons except as related to the body of the State" (*EP*, ii, 154–155/259–260). It is by way of overt example, rather than covert manipulation, that this perception is acquired publicly. For "when upright magistrates, grown gray in dignity" teach justice they "will train their virtual successors" and inspire the "virtue of citizens" (*EP*, I, 154–155/261).

Inside of a well-governed polity public education or the "teaching of justice" is "the state's most important business" and one of the "fundamental maxims of popular or legitimate government" (*EP*, ii, 156/261;156/260–261). More than anything else, it is such teaching that prepares the country's virtual successors for legislative and political self-rule. Rejecting the "monstrously perfect" statutes that were emblematic of Sparta's efforts to guide morals, those who assume this lofty responsibility should never resort to fear or violence to impart such teachings.[7]

How individuals perceive their duties as citizens living inside of a just community is what is most significant, according to Rousseau. It is owing to the variability of this perception, specifically, that the activity of law*making* remains indeterminate despite its predictability. With regards to this indeterminacy, if indeed the lawgiver's art were to manipulate or engineer the outcome of the popular vote than it would not matter whether "each voted for all" or anybody cared that they would be affected by the laws personally.

---

[7] *DSA*, II, 18/24.

Any reciprocal procedures to help realize justice would be redundant or, at best, manifest solely to supplement external maneuverings. Yet this is exactly the opposite of what Rousseau describes in the *Social Contract*; it is the opposite of his emphasis on the need for well-structured and systematically balanced institutions to achieve self-governance. His belief is that citizens will develop a "perception of justice" by voting for laws that affect everyone mutually. Each citizen will pass good laws because the act of voting has rendered him aware of his responsibilities to those persons who are affected by his decisions. Beyond his countrymen such errors will impact upon his friends, his family and himself.

Interestingly, it is in this way that the laws' transparency can be said to be enhanced by the people's ability to accept or reject initiatives at the time of the vote. Of this choice, according to Rousseau, when a law is rejected it is not the people themselves who are mistaken but, rather, the *lawgiver* who was in error as he drafted legislation without knowing whether or not it corresponded to the general will. Remarkably, Rousseau writes that popular rejection of the lawgiver's proposals is not always a bad thing because "if the Legislator makes a mistake about his object and adopts a different principle from the one arising from the nature of things" then "the Laws will imperceptibly weaken, the constitution will be altered, and the State will not cease being agitated until it is either destroyed or changed, and invincible nature has regained its Dominion" (*MG*, II:vi, 116/333). On such occasions it is the sovereign who proves to be the state's savior and no matter what the outcome of the vote "the greatest force of the whole" is felt.

This idea is vividly illustrated by the example of Moses' difficulties at guiding the ancient Israelites out of Egypt. A "stiff-necked" people, the "ancient Israelites changed their minds more than once about whether to follow their would-be lawgiver or rededicate themselves to other leaders and gods" (Exodus 34:9). For Rousseau, at the origin of the state "the true lawgiver (prophet, god) is no more clearly identifiable by the 'people' than is the general will" and "it is up to the people themselves to accept or reject his advances."[8] The example of the ancient Israelites can be shown to inform his view of lawgiving because, in the end, the Jews still chose to follow Moses without their being any less "stiff-necked." Indeed, if it had been the case that Moses had made "a mistake about his object" or adopted "a different principle from the one arising from the nature of things" then his followers may have decided to remain as slaves in Egypt until the arrival of the true prophet. To do otherwise would have been contrary to nature and God.

According to the philosopher this is why "the true Legislator's science" is a science of *which* laws are best for *which* people, rather than being merely a science concerning moral laws generally. Rousseau fears the possibility of imprudent or wrongful legislation being initiated by a lawgiver who makes "a mistake about his object" regardless of their probity. Although the ratifying of each law ought to be wholly unproblematic there will be significant obstacles to this end if the subject-matter at hand is poorly chosen in relation to its object. Of this relationship, the laws must be adapted to the people rather than vice versa as the lawgiver's "problem is to adapt this code to the People for which it is made and to the things about which it decrees" (*LA*, 299/61). No matter how salutary a law code may appear it will be discarded by a people if it is contrary to its character or given situation. For Rousseau, such a rejection can be beneficial politically because not every lawgiver is blessed with the wisdom or foresight to draft laws appropriate to every people or situation.

Contrary to appearances, a "no" vote is sometimes a good thing if the result receives a high proportional majority of voters. In a poorly governed state a debauched citizenry only *rarely* votes in very high numbers until a state is at its ultimate end. Between a state's birth and death, the existence of large proportional majorities reveals much about its political health. When a high percentage of the citizenry strikes down an initiative it usually means that the

---

[8] Honig, "Between Decision and Deliberation," 6.

lawgiver, rather than the people, was mistaken. Rousseau believes that only when a people is *wholly* corrupt can there be unanimity, otherwise, such a consensus is rare in an ailing state.

RELIGION AND VOTE RIGGING

One of the most controversial aspects of the philosopher's political theory is his proposal for a civil religion. According to one line of commentary, Rousseau is said to collapse law into religion by recommending heretics be punished by death for not believing in "the existence of a powerful, intelligent, beneficent, foresighted, and providential Divinity; the afterlife; the happiness of the just; the punishment of the wicked; the sanctity of the Social Contract and the Laws" (*CS*, IV:viii, 222–223/467–468). A hurried afterthought to his more developed ruminations on the lawgiver, supposedly, Book IV:viii of the *Social Contract* might be best described as the Genevan's equivalent to Plato's Myth of Er: a cynical means to procuring justice and obedience to law when the fancifully ineffectual mechanisms of state come up short. For those individuals who cannot be moved by colorful spectacle or talking parrots something more ominous is required: a descending into the fires of Hell.

Placing this threat aside for a moment, it is possible to argue that careful attention to what the Genevan actually says about the relationship between politics and religion in the *Social Contract* demonstrates a more complex dynamic at work. At the end of Book II:vii, for example, he is explicit that "one must not conclude" that "politics and religion have a common object for us, but rather that at the origin of nations, one serves as an instrument of the other" (*CS*, II:vii, 157/384). With respect to voting this absence of a "common object" can be argued to evince a degree of political freedom that would not be possible if the two constructs were construed as being identical. Of this liberty, beyond a few key dogmas chosen to promote good citizenship (and ward off sectarian strife), there is no substantive religious slate to be voted on by individuals who live in a just state. A medium of social order, primarily, the dogmas of the civil religion are intended to entrench and preserve the laws rather than to define their content. Each dogma is to secure justice without giving content to a domain that is and must be the exclusive realm of the sovereign.

In the *Social Contract*, Rousseau does not propose a theocracy and he rejects any appeal to Biblical revelation to buttress the maxims of the lawgiver. In Book IV:viii, Rousseau makes plain that there are not any express maxims to be adhered to beyond the minimalist set of beliefs that he recommends as necessary to sustain good citizenship. Unlike Plato's system, where subjects are indoctrinated into the reality of an idiosyncratically hierarchical form of political organization, individuals in Rousseau's state are taught to fear God and to tolerate each other and to adhere to the laws solely. Of the latter, he is vulnerable to the charge of not having sufficient faith in his own political program (its secular aspects), but he cannot be condemned for appealing to revelation to induce fear to erect a political order.

In this vein, any proposed civil religion should be understood to be an instrument in support of the laws and, less directly, morals, but one that is distinct to its object.[9] Every "human Government is limited by its nature to civil duties" and "when a man serves the State well, he does not owe an account to anyone of the manner in which he serves God" (*letter to Voltaire*, 119/1072).

---

[9] From this relationship, it is apparent that, unlike theocratic rule in which a religious elite is solely responsible for defining and interpreting morals, in Rousseau's system the potential for change to the general will can be demonstrated to necessarily transform certain votes into plebiscites regarding the *moeurs* that underpin certain laws. This may be witnessed when citizens draft a criminal code, for example, as the popular *moeurs* of the community are given expression in a format that is variable (and open to rejection). Laws might be revealed to be more or less conservative or liberal depending upon the changing status of *moeurs* and in ways that may be apparent yet not wholly crystallized within the public mind prior to the vote. In this respect, although morals can never be the subject of legislation, at least indirectly, public morals may be judged by the laws' success. When bad laws are rejected it may be that morals too are bad and when citizens vote for new legislation it may be revelatory of shift in public sentiment regarding morals or emblematic of moral decline.

Relatedly, the philosopher's view is also that the laws that everybody ought to be "bound to admit" should never be permitted to extend beyond any general "principles of morality and natural right" (*letter to Voltaire*, 119/1073). Of such principles, the assertion by some critics that any placing of words into the mouths "of the immortals" inevitably undermines the "free vote of the people" can be challenged because, as Rousseau makes plain, neither a parrot nor its trainer has "the right or the interest to prescribe to others how to think" (*CS*, IV:viii, 222/467–468). He is emphatic that "the man I call *truthful*" will "scarcely have scruples about amusing a group of people with contrived facts from which no unjust judgment results, either for or against anyone living or dead. But every speech which leads to profit or hurt, esteem or scorn, praise or blame for someone, contrary to justice and truth, is a lie which will never approach his heart, his mouth, or his pen" (*RPS*, IV, 33–34/1031). It is inconsequential that a wise lawgiver cannot actually hear the whisperings of a parakeet so long as what the people imagine this bird to be saying is, in the end, essentially true.[10]

Of this truth, similar to Hobbes, he endeavors to promote political tolerance by refashioning personal faith to make it compatible with religious diversity by, among other things, inculcating "sentiments of sociability without which it would be impossible to be a good Citizen or a faithful subject" (*letter to Voltaire*, 119/1072; *CS*, II:vii, 156/383–384).[11] It is the failure of earlier secular solutions to the problem of religious stasis or factionalism that necessitates

---

[10] Kelly comments that Rousseau's view is that such religious duplicities for political gain rarely succeed anyhow. He writes that "the legislator's use of religion cannot be reduced to the reliance on contrived miracles" because "they are inadequate for the legislator's purpose." Reliance upon miracles merely leaves the people "the dupe of the first imposter to appear with a talking bird ... the use of miracles is like the use of force in that only the most recent application is effective. The legislator requires a more enduring effect if he wishes to preserve his institutions." Christopher Kelly, *Rousseau As Author*, Chicago and London: The University of Chicago Press, 2003, 65.

[11] In *Leviathan*, subjects may not brand their neighbors as religious heretics evil or violators of the natural laws. God is a *spirit incorporeal* whose definition is unintelligible to man and it is the sovereign alone who is responsible for

the presence of such sentiments to engender religious concord and good citizenship.

He asserts that each citizen must be willing to accept the Savoyard vicar's belief in the duality of substances or notion that matter is incapable of independent motion in the absence of any divine intelligence. All must be taught how the laws are the "celestial voice that tells each citizen the precepts of public reason" and be willing to sacrifice himself for the good of the community. For those "who are convinced that the divine voice called the whole human Race to the enlightenment and happiness of celestial Intelligences" will "respect the sacred bonds of Societies of which they are members" and "will scrupulously obey the Laws, and the men who are their Authors and Ministers" (*EP*, 146/248; *DSA*, 79–80n/207n).

By convincing men that a bird can commune with the divine the lawgiver will be able to help those who are dazzled by a "love of the beautiful" to hear this celestial voice. Such persons will be able to adopt laws that conform to the general will even when they are unmoved "by human prudence" or incapable of comprehending the utterances of this voice clearly. Ultimately, the logic of Rousseau's theory is such that the ends toward which citizens' vote will be transparent even if the rationale that underpins them is left intentionally opaque.

---

interpreting the natural laws and defining the difference between good and evil. Rousseau objects to this role existing even in the hands of the state beyond support for those interests immediately related to the good of the community (see *Leviathan*, I, xii, 7; xxix, 6; II, xxxi). Rousseau's most famous defense of religious liberty is in his letter to Voltaire from August 18, 1756, where he forcefully remarks "I am indignant that the faith of everyone is not in the most perfect liberty, and that man dares control the interior of consciences where he is unable to penetrate ... Have the Kings of this world any superintendency in the other? And have they any right to torment their Subjects here below in order to force them to go to Paradise? No; all human Government is limited by its nature to civil duties; and whatever the Sophist Hobbes might have been able to say on this, when a man serves the State well, he does not owe an account to anyone of the manner in which he serves God" (*letter to Voltaire*, 119/1072).

THE GENERAL WILL AND PUBLIC OPINION

The outcome of any vote is unknowable prior to the official casting of ballots or show of hands.[12] Although, the direction or sway of the general will ought to be *claire* and *lumineuses* always, Rousseau is explicit that "one can never be assured that a private will is in conformity with the general will until it has been submitted" to the assembly *(CS*, II: vii, 156/383). Such uncertainty remains, in part, because the vagaries of *l'opinion publique* can upset the vote at any time.[13]

According to the theory of the *Social Contract* it is not opinion but *will* that is ratified into law and it is impossible to discern the differences between the two until after all of the ballots (or hands) have been counted. Even afterwards it is sometimes difficult to discern any differences between the two and an observer can only know whether the one or the other has been ratified by the fractiousness of deliberations or the polarity of the vote's final tally. Unlike the general will which is a rational and universal expression of the common good, public opinion is always a reflection of the personal preferences of individuals in society or the "partial associations" of the larger community. Opinion is marked by its variability and subjectivity rather than by the certainty, universality and permanence of the general will.[14] Opinion is capricious and unpredictable while the

---

12 Ideally, voting is by a show of hands unless the size of an assembly renders this impossible or unfeasible. In this book, I usually discuss voting in terms of ballots.

13 This lack of clarity can be witnessed in the *Letter to Alembert*, for example, where the term that Rousseau employs, *les opinions publiques*, is pluralized in a way that is incompatible with its usage in his later political writings. Unfortunately, for English readers, the most important passages identifying the concept's distinctive features have been mistranslated in a number of popular translations rendering the concept expressly singular ("*l' opinion publique*") and, to a degree, something entirely other than what Rousseau intended. For example, see Bloom, *Politics and the Arts: Letter to M. Alembert on the Theatre*, Ithaca: Cornell University Press, 1960. Bloom alternates between the singular and the plural throughout his translation. The key passage describing opinion's resistance to reason or force (p. 74) is plural.

14 French historian Mona Ozouf emphasizes the slippery nature of this construct in Rousseau's philosophy, writing that "definitions of public opinion in Rousseau varied considerably. One could garner a good many passages from his writings in which *l'estime public* or *le murmure public* served as barriers to

general will is an entity that is always "constant, unalterable, and pure" (*CS*, IV:I, 199/438). The latter exists as a succession of discrete moments but such temporal spaces are marked by a regularity of which, unlike opinion, flux is the exception.

In the *Social Contract* opinion's capriciousness poses a danger to the actualization of the general will but, in an ironic twist, perhaps, this trait also serves to impede efforts to manipulate the general will by traditional methods of political control. Although, "the common good is clearly apparent everywhere, and requires only good sense to be perceived," it nevertheless remains the case that "countless unforeseen circumstances" can influence such good sense unduly. Rousseau asserts that it is always "passion that leads us" (*DI*, I, 27/143; *E*, II, 80–81/304–305; *FP*, XVI:i, 70/554; *N*, 188/962) especially with respect to public opinion (*LA*, 300/62; *CS*, IV:vii, 215/458; *CGP*, 175–176/961; *PC*, 153/937; *RPS*, VIII, 71/1077) and inside even the best of states the vagaries of this fickle medium make the vote always uncertain. The presence of such caprice reveals why, as a possibility, "one can never be assured that a private will is in conformity with the general will" until balloting or voting is over despite the absence of any "tangled contradictory interests." Opinion's vulnerability to "unforeseen circumstances" renders it "very mobile and changing" with a randomness that makes it difficult to predict.[15] Despite the usual or expected consistency of the general will every vote has

despotism or in which public opinion had a valuable supervisory and regulatory function ... but there are also a good many texts in which the tendency of public opinion to crystallize in cliques or in special interest associations rendered it immediately suspect ... Rousseau ... foresaw that its underlying nature was to shatter into different representations. Thus it had not the least infallibility and needed constant rectification." Mona Ozouf, "'Public Opinion' at the End of the Old Regime", *Journal of Modern History* 60, suppl., September 1988, S4–S9.

[15] In the *Letter to Alembert* the term *les opinions publiques* is described as both the subject of *partent* and *amènent* to emphasize how onerous it is to manage (and how difficult it is to manipulate) in the face of "chance, countless accidental causes" and "countless unforeseen circumstances" (*LA*, 305/68). "Les opinions publiques, quoique si difficiles à gouverner, sont pourtant par elles-mêmes très mobiles et changeantes. Le hasard, mille causes fortuites, mille circonstances imprévues, font ce que la force et la raison ne sauroient faire: ou plutôt c'est précisément parce que le hasard les dirige que la force n'y peut rien;

the potential for surprise because "whatever impulsion is given" to opinion, as an accidental force, "does not bring up the desired point more easily" (*LA*, 305/68).

Correspondingly, Rousseau comments that even the most convincing rhetorician is incapable of total political indoctrination. Human willing can be validated or reinforced by outsiders, such as a wise lawgiver, but it can never be wholly imposed from without because of the vicissitudes that accompany human emotions. *Ennemis de l'opinion* can influence belief in a "methodical and consistent spirit" but only so far as such belief adheres to a trajectory toward which it was already predisposed. This idea is captured by Rousseau's eloquent condemnation of the theater in the *Letter to Alembert* where he asserts that no one should attribute to it "the power to change sentiments or morals, which it can only follow and embellish" (*LA*, 264/17–18). In the theater audience-members must be already predisposed to the sentiments and emotions being acted out on stage for a performance to be successful. He stresses that audience-members can never be emotionally affected by a performance unless the actors have understood and interpreted their sentiments clearly. For "rather than giving the law to the public, the theatre receives the law from it" (*LA*, 266/21) and, as Allan Bloom comments, in the theater playwrights become "entirely dependent" upon their audience "for the style and subject matter of their presentation."[16] In "choosing the passions which he presents as attractive," the playwright "cannot follow his wishes but must accept ours."[17] Our wishes must be honored for this relationship to persist because "the theatre can only succeed when it touches what is really wanted."[18]

---

comme les dés qui partent de la main, quelque impulsion qu' on leur donne n'en amènent pas plus aisément le point désiré" (*LA*, 305/368).

[16] Bloom, *Politics and the Arts*, xxiii.

[17] Bloom, *Politics and the Arts*, xxiv.

[18] Bloom, *Politics and the Arts*, xxiii. The spirit of this idea was not lost on Tocqueville who observes that "public opinion has a strange power" that "by some mighty pressure of the mind" imposes "its ideas and makes them penetrate men's very souls." In *Democracy in America*, trans. G. Lawrence, ed. J.P., Mayer, New York: Harper and Row, 1969 [1835], 435.

Inside of a just state it is owing to this psychological predisposition that Rousseau's lawgiver can be said to persuade citizens by way of emotive imagery and affective speech, but never *convince* anyone into adopting any legal measure. It is not only that rational convincing is useless for making "a blind multitude" perceive "objects as they are, or sometimes as they should appear to be" (*CS*, II:vi, 154/380) but, critically, this status serves to preserve the integrity of the sovereign's vote by allowing citizens to remain independent from the domination of reason.[19] Unchained from any rigid imperatives Rousseau's citizens are free to reject any initiative owing to their predilection toward subjectivity. Such a disposition makes it possible for the lawgiver to teach "moral truths"[20] in a way that need not be interpreted categorically or able to produce only a single answer.

Of this restriction, it is not coincidental that the exact limits that Rousseau places upon the lawgiver's methods in Book II, ch. VII of the *Social Contract* are identical to the types of resistance that he ascribes to opinion in the *Letter to Alembert*. In the later work the lawgiver's methods can be shown to correspond to the susceptibilities attributed to opinion in the earlier writing nearly verbatim illuminating their barriers. Rousseau writes that the lawgiver is "unable to use either *force or reasoning*" and, in the *Letter to Alembert*, "countless unforeseen circumstances do what *force and reason* could not" when guiding opinion (*CS*, II:vii, 156/383; *LA*, 305/68; my italics). In a just state citizens are free to reject any legislative initiative, in part, because the subjectivity of this *autorité d'un autre ordre* restricts the means by which the lawgiver can "transform human nature." Importantly, this seminal distinction between non-rational *persuading* and rational *convincing* is indispensable to political autonomy because it is *raison* together with its opposite that ultimately determines the outcome of the popular vote. Right

---

[19] Christopher Kelly, "To Persuade Without Convincing," *American Journal of Political Science* 31 (2) May 1987: 321–335.

[20] Kelly, "To Persuade Without Convincing," 324.

supplants appetite when each "consults his reason before heeding his inclinations" (CS, I:viii, 141/364) to create "an admirable agreement between interest and justice" (CS, II:iv, 149/374). Men consult reason *before* their inclinations but never instead of them. Together, it is both reason and inclination that are heeded and such a confluence is "admirable" because it is not only just but also free.

VOTING AND ROME

Rousseau's analysis of Roman governance in Book IV:iv of the *Social Contract* is sometimes said to betray a wider elitist streak in his political thought than he is willing to admit. According to John P. McCormick, for example, "at crucial if neglected junctures of his magnum opus, Rousseau fairly explicitly prescribes institutions that enable rather than constrain the prerogative of elites within republics and popular governments." Through "sociologically anonymous principles like generality and popular sovereignty, and by confining elite accountability to elections alone, Rousseau's institutional analyses and proposals allow, nay encourage, wealthier citizens and magistrates to dominate the politics of popular governments in semi-surreptitious and unassailable ways."[21] Examining the stipulations of the Emperor Servius that he praises so highly, McCormick argues that the philosopher justifies weighted voting for the wealthy within sovereign assemblies like Rome's centuriate assembly (comitia centuriata) in order to create an intra-institutional balancing of democracy (or rule by the poor.) When the wealthiest citizens are in agreement in the assembly the numbers of votes allotted to them

---

[21] John P. McCormick, "Rousseau's Rome and the Repudiation of Populist Republicanism," *Critical Review of International Social and Political Philosophy*, 10 (1) March 2007: 3–27. For alternative readings of Rousseau's ideas on Roman institutions see C.E. Vaughan, *The Political Writings of Jean-Jacques Rousseau*, vol. II, Cambridge: Cambridge University Press, 1915, 109; Charles Hendel, *Jean-Jacques Rousseau, Moralist*, vol. II, London and Oxford: Oxford University Press, 1934, 224–226; R.D. Masters, *The Political Philosophy of Rousseau*, Princeton: Princeton University Press, 1968, 305–306; Richard Fralin, *Rousseau and Representation: a Study of the Development of his Concept of Political Institutions*, New York: Columbia University Press, 1978, 113; Melzer, *The Natural Goodness of Man*, 237n.

can settle all issues – only when their votes are split does vote-counting continue such that the poorest citizens have any say at all in Rome. Following Rome's example, Rousseau's endorsement of the centuriate assembly is said to allow the smallest majority of wealthy citizens within to decide legislative questions without the vote ever devolving to the ranks of the majority of (the poorest) citizens.

With McCormick, I agree that careful attention to Rousseau's detailed analysis and praise of Roman institutions is germane to any proper understanding of his political theory. This said, it is unclear to me that the philosopher indeed "uses Rome prescriptively rather than descriptively" or that the political lessons that he draws are as unassailably elitist as may appear.[22] Of the latter, it is worthwhile to note that, at least according to one pre-eminent authority on the subject, the centuriate assembly was not the locus of political power or, more significantly, sovereignty in republican Rome. Although it is indeed true that "throughout Roman history the ruling nobility was intent on de-emphasizing the democratic element of the constitution, as convincingly testified by the composition, structure and voting technique of the assemblies," according to Karl Loewenstein,

> the Roman assemblies were never regarded, or regarded
> themselves, as the sovereign policy-making organ of the state.
> Indispensable as they were for the designation of leaders
> by annual elections, in the legislative field their role, if
> constitutionally required, was secondary in comparison with
> the Senate and the magistrates who, between themselves,
> monopolized the policy-making function. The assemblies were
> an essential cogwheel in the machinery of the political process;
> but different from Greece, they were never the fulcrum of
> political power.[23]

[22] McCormick, "Rousseau's Rome and the Repudiation of Populist Republicanism," 9.
[23] Karl Loewenstein, *The Governance of Rome*, The Hague: Martinus Nijhoff, 1973, 130.

Of Rome's actual fulcrum, Loewenstein explains that until its final degeneration the Senate was usually populated not by a wealthy elite but by "a collective body of civilian-military professionals" who were prepossessed by "a deep sense of patriotic responsibility and national mission." Unsurprisingly, perhaps, those senators who were a wealthy elite within this rarified body were "affluent enough to place the honor of the office above gain, and patriotic enough not to equate the national interest with the advancement of their class interests."[24]

Of this self-checking of class interests, it is striking how closely Loewenstein's account of the impulses guiding Rome's senate mirrors Rousseau's own description of elective aristocracy (where natural virtue is more politically material than wealth). Beyond this similarity, though, it is equally striking how much Loewenstein's account of the Republic's diminished assembly deviates from anything remotely resembling sovereign authority in the *Social Contract*. Although, "the Roman assemblies were never regarded, or regarded themselves, as the sovereign policy-making organ in the state," the same cannot be said to be true for the sovereign assembly in Rousseau's state. At every turn, the philosopher emphasizes the political primacy of the people or, what he speaks of elsewhere when personally addressing Geneva's *Conseil général*, the city-state's "magnificent, most honored and sovereign lords" (*Dedicatory Letter to DI*, 11/121). Rousseau not only describes this collective body as being the sole sovereign organ in a just *patrie* and Geneva but he empowers it to make laws that, unlike executive decrees, cannot be either directly or indirectly rescinded or repealed by any other branch of the state.

With respect to Rousseau's thoughts on the influence of the wealthy within the divisions in the Roman Centuries, according to the *Social Contract* such divisions were "only made practicable by the simple morals of the early Romans, their disinterestedness,

---

[24] Loewenstein, *The Governance of Rome*, 147, 152.

their taste for agriculture, their disdain for commerce and for the desire for profit" (*CS*, IV:iv, 206/448). Of such simple morals, he finds Rome's wealthy elite to be constrained by the same republican virtues generally attributed to the Senate at its height by Loewenstein and his conclusion, as Masters reminds us, is that "factual inequalities of status and wealth are perfectly consistent with a solid regime provided they cannot be used on a personal basis to make some citizens dependent on others."[25] Arguably, it is such a dependency that would be created by allowing a wealthy elite to dominate the sovereign assembly of a just state in "semi-surreptitious ways." Unlike a ruling class that is marked by a "devouring greed" that arrives at decisions according to its own class interests, according to Rousseau "it must be carefully noted that morals and censorship, which were stronger than this institution, corrected its vices in Rome, and that a given rich man could find himself relegated to the class of the poor if he made too great a display of his wealth" (*CS*, IV:iv, 207/448).

Of the second question of how much or how little Rome's institutions ought to serve as a model for a just or legitimate state, McCormick is correct that Rousseau says that "the history of the Roman regulations" will "explain more tangibly all the maxims I could establish" (*CS*, IV:iii, 203/443). On the face of it, though, I believe that this key line can be interpreted in two ways of which one is merely to highlight how much the Republic's example ought to inform or, as Rousseau writes, "explain" his political maxims without making any wholesale prescriptions. McCormick cites this same passage to opposite effect and his reading of the closing of Book IV:iii may indeed be the more accurate but, at the very least, it should be noted that significant aspects of Roman governance were rejected by Rousseau. As he describes in *Political Economy* and the *Social Contract*, at times, Roman statecraft was

---

[25] Masters, *The Political Philosophy of Rousseau*, 390.

non-ideal and deleterious to stable rule because the proper domain
between sovereign and executive rule injudiciously overlapped (and
ought not to be placed underneath any banner of revivable Roman
institutions). More bluntly, Derathé's view is that the entire section on Rome in Book IV:iv of the *Social Contract* is little more
than filler: "in reality, it was for Rousseau a matter of filling out
this Fourth Book, even at the price of a digression so that he could
insert the chapter on Civil Religion."[26] Whether or not this dismissive reading is accurate, and I find it to be an overstatement, it is
certain that Rome was as much of a divided model for Rousseau as
Geneva.

WILL-FORMATION AND LIBERTY IN THE
SOCIAL CONTRACT

Since the late eighteenth century the charge of psychological conditioning is one of the most ubiquitous criticisms leveled against
Rousseau's political thought. Together with accusations of collectiv-
ism, majoritarianism and totalitarianism, undue manipulation or
"hegemonic conditioning" can be said to top the list of abuses that
readers ascribe to the philosopher. With a familiar ring, allegations
once voiced by Joseph de Maistre, Benjamin Constant and Edmund
Burke can be heard echoing from the pages of mid twentieth-century
authors such as J.W. Chapman, J.L. Talmon, Lester G. Crocker and,
more recently, Steven Johnston.[27] Caveats aside, I have attempted in
this chapter to illuminate and, to an extent, refute this enduring
criticism by revealing how such allegations are undermined by the
various organic and institutional elements in Rousseau's system.
Ideally, lawmaking in his *patrie* ought not to be an end-product of

---

[26] *Pléiade*, III, 1495, cited in Masters, *The Political Philosophy of Rousseau*, n305.
[27] Johnston, *Encountering Tragedy*, 87. From the past, see Irving Babbitt, *Rousseau
and Romanticism*, New York: Houghton Mifflin, 1919; Chapman, *Rousseau,
Totalitarian or Liberal?*; Talmon, *The Origins of Totalitarian Democracy*; Lester
Crocker, "Introduction," in *Jean-Jacques Rousseau: The Social Contract and
Discourse on Inequality*, New York: Simon and Schuster, 1967, xvii.

hegemonic conditioning even when a "partial and moral existence" supplants "the physical and independent existence we have all received from nature." To forge or preserve such an existence the philosopher neither suggests nor prescribes a total loss of political control by the people at any time during the lifecycle of any legitimate state.

4   Popular sovereignty and the republican fear of large assemblies

According to Jeremy Waldron, "the clear consensus in the canon of legal and political thought" is "that the size of a legislative body is an obstacle, rather than an advantage, to rational decisionmaking" and, as such, large assemblies give rise to "jurisprudential unease about legislation." Originating "in ancient prejudice that surfaced during the Enlightenment," the source of this unease is said to be that "legislation is not just deliberate, administrative, or political: it is, above all, in the modern world, the product of an *assembly* – the many, the multitude, the rabble (or their representatives)."[1] Within this canonical consensus large assemblies are said to be irrational and occasionally demagogic because they are endowed with traits more characteristic of a rabble than of a selectively chosen self-legislating elite.

This description by Waldron is given substance in the writings of a number of eighteenth- and nineteenth-century theorists of representative government as well as critics of democracy during the early part of the twentieth century. According to David Hume, for example, "all numerous assemblies, however composed, are mere mob."[2] Similarly, James Madison writes that in "all very numerous assemblies, of whatever characters composed, passion never fails to wrest the sceptre from reason. Had every Athenian citizen been a

---

[1] Jeremy Waldron, *The Dignity of Legislation*, Cambridge: Cambridge University Press, 1999, 31–32.
[2] David Hume, "Idea of a Perfect Commonwealth," in Eugene F. Miller, ed., *Essays: Moral, Political and Literary*, Indianapolis: Liberty Press, 1985 [1889], 523.

Socrates; every Athenian assembly would still have been a mob."[3] Large elected legislatures are a rabble, according to Madison, because "the more multitudinous a representative assembly may be rendered, the more ... ignorance will be the dupe of cunning; and passion the slave of sophistry and declamation."[4] Articulating a near-identical view, a generation later John Stuart Mill asserts that "a numerous assembly is as little fitted to the direct business of legislation as for that of administration."[5] Likewise, in the twentieth century an author of a very different persuasion, Gaetano Mosca, argues that although "an assembly of representatives is never a 'mob,' in the sense of being a haphazard, inorganic assemblage of human beings," it is still manifestly dangerous because legislators' "personal ambitions and party interests" make it inevitable that government will be dominated by self-opportunistic elites.[6]

Each of these authors offers wide-ranging and sometimes contradictory explanations for why large legislatures are inherently fractious and unstable yet concur in their basic conclusions. Each differs on whether it is large majorities or simply majority rule that is most problematic and for what reasons. Although not all reject the latter, democracy's basic principle, each believes that large assemblies in one way or another pose a danger to rational lawmaking. For each of these thinkers there are thoughtful reasons why this ought not to be true owing to the myriad benefits or virtues embodied by representative government and yet all remain convinced that increases in numbers produce mob rule. Many find this to be the case not only for unqualified or popular majorities but, as Madison remarks, for "*all* very numerous assemblies, of *whatever* characters composed"

[3] James Madison, Alexander Hamilton and John Jay, *The Federalist*, Philadelphia: The Franklin Library [1788] 1977, No. 55, 401.

[4] *Federalist*, No. 58, 424–425.

[5] John Stuart Mill, "Considerations on Representative Government," in John Gray, ed. and intro., *On Liberty and Other Essays*, Oxford: Oxford University Press, 1991 [1861], 5, 277.

[6] Gaetano Mosca, *The Ruling Class*, trans. Hannah D. Kahn, New York and London: McGraw-Hill, 1939, 257, 259.

(my italics). Regardless of selection criteria or other aristocratic features, numbers alone are said to be able to reduce an assembly of "Socrates" to a rabble.

But is this true? Is it indeed the case that high numbers necessarily diminish the political competency of exceedingly large assemblies? Must the rationality of decisionmaking necessarily decline in a forum of hundreds or even of thousands? Long taken as self-evident, this question is one of the most enduring criticisms of democracy since its emergence in fourth-century Athens. As Waldron notes, it is also one of the most persistent criticisms of modern representative government generally.[7] In this chapter, I explore this question from the standpoint of one of the few modern republican thinkers to defend lawmaking by excessively large assemblies: Jean-Jacques Rousseau. Examining his thoughts on the relationship between numbers and legislative rationality, specifically, I argue that, unlike Madison or Mill, Rousseau is unique for his willingness to accept lawmaking by great or extended majorities. Critically, I show that in his *Social Contract, Letters Written From The Mountain* and later practical political writings, the chief danger to liberty is not assemblies of "any character composed" but assemblies of poorly composed character. Examining the philosopher's belief that size poses a marginal threat to decisionmaking, I explain why Rousseau's political theory is the only one to offer a solution to the danger of numbers as a source of this enduring "jurisprudential unease about legislation." Contrary to the eighteenth and early nineteenth-century caricatures of the Genevan as a utopian democrat, I show how Rousseau's solution to the danger of high numbers also evinces an historical sensibility to the problems that afflict decisionmaking by large majorities that, in many ways, situates his political philosophy closer to the larger republican tradition he opposes than may appear from his famous defense of popular sovereignty.

---

[7] Waldron, *The Dignity of Legislation*, 31–32.

ATHENS AND THE REPUBLICAN FEAR
OF LARGE MAJORITIES

Ancient critics of democracy in fourth-century Athens identify a litany of debilitating social and political vices that render rule by "the Many" unstable. In no special order these are:

1 political amateurism;
2 a wrong standard for justice as a governing principle;
3 excessive love of equality;
4 rule by the poor;
5 the absence of a middle class;
6 inefficiency;
7 simple government; and
8 minority domination and/or majoritarian tyranny.

According to political historians and theorists such as Mogens Herman Hansen, Karl Loewenstein, Ernest Barker, among others, each of these vices represents the most salient criticisms of democracy leveled by Greek authors that, in later centuries, were voiced against rulers of the Roman Republic in the years prior to the dictatorship of the Caesars.[8] Athens' most trenchant critic was, of course, Plato, but much more recent political thinkers articulate compelling and expansive accounts of democracy's failings in fourth-century Greece. More than anybody else, it is Plato who offers a critical blueprint for all later rejectionists of rule by the Many owing to, among other things, his vivid metaphor of democracy as a fearful, friendless "many-headed beast"[9] made tyrannical by passion and an insatiable love of equality.

---

[8] Mogens Herman Hansen, *The Athenian Democracy in the Age of Demosthenes*, trans. J.A. Crook, Norman, OK: Oklahoma University Press, 1999, 175–177; Karl Loewenstein, *The Governance of Rome*, The Hague: Martinus Nijhoff, 1973, 262–273; Ernest Barker, *The Political Thought of Plato and Aristotle*, New York: Dover Publications, 1959, 173–174, 459–460. Also see Jennifer Tolbert Roberts, *Athens on Trial: The Antidemocratic Tradition in Western Thought*, Princeton: Princeton University Press, 1994, 158–166; R.K. Sinclair, *Democracy and Participation in Athens*, Cambridge: Cambridge University Press, 1988, 211–218; A.H.M. Jones, *Athenian Democracy*, Baltimore: Johns Hopkins University Press, 1986 [1957], 41–72.

[9] Plato, *The Republic*, trans. Allan Bloom, New York: Basic Books, 1968, 588c–589b, 271–272.

According to the author of *The Republic*, this many-headed beast is rule by the fractious poor who know little of the science of politics or the standards of justice that are to guide the state.[10] A source of war and stasis in the *polis*, the perils of democracy originate not only with differences of class but also increases of size: the sheer number of voters or lawmakers or *demos* who participate in governance is destabilizing. Conferring political power to a broad swath of the citizenry, such as the Athenian *ekklesia* (with a quorum of 6,000), for example, allows differences of wealth, tribe, occupation and martial status, among other distinctions, to divide political rule. Soldiers, artisans, farmers, merchants and seafarers, among other Athenians of varying degrees of political skill, were all permitted a voice at the Pnyx. "Many cities but not a city" (*Rep.*, 423a, 100), such diversity was, in part, the ineluctable consequence of the especially high numbers who participate in lawmaking. Unlike the perfect unity of a regime guided by the Forms this gross franchise was seen as elevating those least adept at governing into a political role that ultimately brought about the destruction of the state (*Rep.*, 420e–421a, 98).

This criticism of Athens recapitulates a similar view articulated a half a century earlier by Herodotus who equates rule by the Many with anarchy. Even more so than Plato, though, Herodotus emphasizes the political dangers that accompany popular decisionmaking by an ignorant and impulsive majority in *The History*. The chief failing of democracy is said to be less the absence of a wise elite, as Plato stresses, than the political problems associated with legislation by a herd-like crowd. Recounting a discussion of the relative merits of the different regime types at a gathering of Persian grandees in 454 BC, Herodotus tells how Magabyzus asserts that "there is nothing stupider, nothing more given to outrage, than a useless mob" as knowledge "does not inhere in the Many" who instead

---

[10] *Republic*, 428d, 106; *Statesman*, trans. Seth Benardete, Chicago: The University of Chicago Press, 1984, 292e293a, III, 45.

"rush into things and push them this way and that without intelligent purposes, like a river in winter spate."[11] Perhaps, the first to equate democracy with dictatorship, Darius replies that "when the Many are rulers ... knavery is bred in the state" for "they combine together to maladminister the public concerns. This goes on until one man takes charge of affairs for the Many and puts a stop to the knaves. As a result of this, he wins the admiration of the Many, and, being so admired, lo! You have your despot again."[12]

A century later, Aristotle also criticizes rule by the Many as a venal form of governance despite its notable mitigating virtues. In the *Politics*, Aristotle writes that democracy and oligarchy are primarily distinguished by differences of wealth[13] yet numbers are secondarily important owing to their effect upon deliberation. Unlike the lessons expounded by his teacher in *The Republic*, Aristotle mentions the special benefits that accompany deliberations by large majorities despite the dangers of democracy. Of the former,

> There is this to be said for the many: each of them by himself
> may not be of a good quality; but when they all come together
> it is possible that they may surpass – collectively and as a body,
> although not individually – the quality of the few best, in much
> the same way that feasts to which many contribute may excel
> those provided at one person's expense.
>
> *(Politics, III:xi, 1281b1, 108)*

It is not only virtue but the judgment of the people that improves with increases in their size:

> When they all meet together, the people display a good enough
> gift of perception, and combined with the better class they are
> of service to the city (just as impure food, when it is mixed with

---

[11] Herodotus, 1987. *The History*, trans. David Grene, Chicago: The University of Chicago Press, 1987, LXXXI, 248.

[12] *Histories*, LXXXII, 249.

[13] Aristotle, *The Politics*, trans. Ernest Barker, intro. R.F. Stalley, New York and Oxford: Oxford University Press, 1995, III:viii, 101; III:viii, 102.

pure, makes the whole concoction more nutritious than a small amount of the pure would be); but each of them is imperfect in the judgments he forms by himself.

(*Politics, III:ix,1281b21, 109–110*)

Owing to these virtues, he believes "it is therefore just that the people should be sovereign on the more important issues, since the assembly, the council, and the court consist of many people" (1282a35, 111). The least worst of all corrupt regime types, according to Aristotle, democracy's benefits are undermined and popular governance made tyrannical when the people are disposed to govern as a "monarchy – a single composite monarch made up of many members, with the many playing the sovereign, not as individuals, but collectively" (*Politics*, IV:iv, 1292a7, 145). Like the oligarchic forger of *De Respublica Atheniensium*, he believes that owing to numbers "flatterers are held in honor" and majority rule "becomes analogous to the tyrannical form of monarchy."[14] Ultimately, the "sovereignty of decrees" supplants "that of laws" and demagogues assume power "since the multitude follows their guidance."[15] Echoing this dire view, two centuries later Polybius warns of a "craving for prominence" or unquenchable need by individuals "to raise themselves above their fellow citizens"[16] that renders rule by the majority inherently unstable.[17]

[14] *Politics*, IV:iv, 145.

[15] *Politics*, IV:iv, 145.

[16] Polybius, *Histories: The Rise of the Roman Empire*, trans. Ian Scott-Kilvert, intro. F.W. Walbank, London: Penguin Books, 1979, IV, 309.

[17] This is also the view of Thomas Aquinas who invokes the memory of Athens to condemn medieval democracy. Popular rule is said to lead to inevitable "dissentions and disputes" as the many are unable to "enjoy peace, justice ... and ... the abundance of wealth." See Aquinas, *De Regimine Principum* in *On Politics and Ethics*, trans. and ed. Paul Sigmund, New York: W.W. Norton and Company, 1988, I, 18. Unlike the future saint, Machiavelli, of course, believes that such dissentions and disputes are a good thing and "the tumults between the nobles and the plebs" the "first cause of keeping Rome free." Yet it was also true, according to this advisor to princes everywhere, that "the restless spirits of the plebs" created "infinite dissentions and scandals in a republic" that helped to weaken rulers and that, in his view, popular republics were also the most "licentious." See Niccolò Machiavelli, *Discourses on Livy*, trans. Harvey C.

Prior to Montesquieu, the most famous modern critic of "great and numerous assemblies" is Thomas Hobbes.[18] More than any European thinker before him, Hobbes writes at length in *De Cive* and the *Elements of Law* about the risks that high numbers pose to parliamentary government, specifically.[19] Although Hobbes does not ascribe every assorted political vice among the "democratical" English to numbers alone,[20] unlike earlier philosophers who emphasize the threats created by other causal agents such as political amateurism, Hobbes gives special weight to numbers. According to the author of *Leviathan*, the difficulties that arise from high numbers are not unique to democracy and can be witnessed in any regime type in which decisionmaking power is shared. What distinguishes rule by the few or the many from monarchy is the problem of decisionmaking by *any* body in possession of multiple opinions.[21] His view is that the greater the number of opinions the worse the decisions rendered.

In the *Elements of Law*, *De Cive* and *Behemoth*, for example, Hobbes uses the terms "great multitude" and "great Assembly" to distinguish demographically large majorities from "lesser Councells"

Mansfield and Nathan Tarcov, London and Chicago: The University of Chicago Press, 1996 [1519], iv, 16; v, 18; ii, 11.

[18] Montesquieu, *Considerations on the Causes of the Greatness of the Romans and their Decline*, trans. and intro. David Lowenthal, New York: The Free Press, 1965 [1734], 93.

[19] Thomas Hobbes, *De Cive* in *The English Works of Thomas Hobbes of Malmesbury*, ed. Sir W. Molesworth, vol. II, London: John Bohn, 1841,V:v, 67; *The Elements of Law [Human Nature, De Corpore Politico]*, ed. Ferdinand Tönnies, intro. M.M. Goldsmith, London: Frank Cass and Co., 1969 [1651], II:i:2, 108–109 [henceforth *EL*] II:i:15, 115; II:ii:1, 118; *Leviathan*, ed. and trans. Edwin Curly, Indianapolis: Hackett, 1994 [1651], XIX:vi, 121, XIX:ix, 122.

[20] According to Hobbes, "divers Innovators innovate divers wayes" (*De Cive*, V:v, 67) and "there ariseth an inconstancy from the number" that renders democracy a constant state of flux. Owing to this inconstancy, the commonwealth is unstable as "the Laws do flote here, and there, as it were upon the waters" (*Leviathan*, XIX:vi, 121; *De Cive*, X:xiii, 139).

[21] Man's psychological egoism precludes anything but a monarchy, according to Hobbes. See Jean Hampton, *Hobbes and the Social Contract Tradition*, Cambridge: Cambridge University Press, 1986, 105; also see Richard E. Flathman, *Thomas Hobbes: Skepticism, Individuality and Chastened Politics*, London: Sage Publications, 1993, 134–157.

in an effort to emphasize the salience of numbers above other attributes (*Elements of Law*, II:v:4, 141–142; II:v:8, 143; *De Cive*, X:x, 136; X:xi, 137; X:xiv, 139; X:xv, 140). This can be seen in the *Elements of Law*, for example, as he collapses any differences between aristocracy and democracy with regard to where power is located and describes the latter's exercise as a problem of *numbers* chiefly. Explaining that the "aptitude to dissolution" is "an inconvenience in such aristocracies only where the affairs of state are debated in great and numerous assemblies," he notes that Athens and Rome were unstable "aristocracies" that were apt to dissolve owing to problems of electoral and, critically, functional scale. Centralizing power in far fewer hands, both Athens and Rome would have been more secure, by Hobbes' account, if the people committed "the handling of state affairs to a few; such as is the aristocracy of Venice at this day" (*Elements of Law*, II:v:8, 143). With respect to foreign relations, "there are many reasons why deliberations are lesse successfull in great Assemblies, than in lesser Councells" as large numbers of advisors are "for the most part unskilfull (that I say not incapable)" at "Forraign Affaires," offering little more than their own "impertinent Opinions" (*De Cive*, X:x, 136–137).

In *Behemoth*, Hobbes' comparison between England and Athens is historically significant because it marks the first time that any modern thinker consciously superimposes the many ancient vices of a popular or unqualified majority upon the qualified.[22] In *Behemoth*, he writes that "both the Rump and all other sovereign assemblies, if they have but one voice, though they be

---

[22] Hanna F. Pitkin comments that "the etymological development in this period is confused, and the available evidence is not conclusive," yet it appears that in Hobbes' writings terms like "represent" were for the first time "applied to the Parliament as an image of the whole nation." Of whether Hobbes was "making a brilliant application, or merely expressing what was the current conception of the terms," Pitkin is uncertain but believes that "the earliest application I have come across of the noun 'representative' to a member of Parliament occurs in 1651" and that "it is also the year in which Hobbes published the *Leviathan*, in the midst of this etymological development." See Hanna Fenichel Pitkin, *The Concept of Representation*, Berkeley: University of California Press, 1967, 250.

many men, yet are they but one person. For contrary commands cannot consist in one and the same voice, which is the voice of the greatest part; and therefore they might govern well enough, if they had honesty and wit enough" (*Behemoth*, IV, 156). Like Hume's belief that "all numerous assemblies" are "mere mob," he believes that large assemblies are deleterious to good statecraft because, at best, men ignore reason in their deliberations and, at worst, degenerate into a rabble.[23]

Accepting the merits of this dire viewpoint as something only slightly less than an historical fact (as Mill later did) it is significant to note that there is, at least, one republican theorist who breaks decisively on this question of size being an insurmountable obstacle to lawmaking by great assemblies. Although cognizant of the political evils associated with high numbers, Rousseau considers these perils to be less worrisome than those originating from other sources existent within smaller lawmaking bodies.

ROUSSEAU ON LARGE ASSEMBLIES AND MOB RULE
Rousseau is unique for his acceptance of voting by unusually large assemblies and the scale that he applies is that of small populations or states – popular majorities infinitely greater than England's Parliament or the representative bodies that Hume or Madison label as "mobs." Steven Johnston writes, for example, "Rousseau's numbers haunt a participatory ethic" asking "How can the citizen perceive the influence that his voice has when it is muted, if not silenced, by the sheer force of numbers?"[24] For the Genevan, this sheer force of numbers only becomes "burdensome," according to Hilail Gildin, when it reaches a level that necessitates the "formation of smaller

---

[23] A century later, Madison echoes this opinion writing that "the more multitudinous a representative assembly may be rendered, the more ... ignorance will be the dupe of cunning; and passion the slave of sophistry and declamation" (*Fed.*, LVIII, 424–425).

[24] Steven Johnston, *Encountering Tragedy: Rousseau and the Project of Democratic Order*, Ithaca: Cornell University Press, 1999, 83.

states out of larger ones."[25] Rousseau accepts, "with reservations, that popular assemblies are more feasible in small states than in larger ones"[26] and his standard for lawmaking is, according to Alfred Cobban, a "tiny state."[27] Within this tiny state the danger to legislation is said to be large pluralities rather than majorities; it is the presence of factions rather than numbers that impedes enunciation of the general will in a body with membership of any size. Unlike in his system, this danger can be checked in a conventional state by keeping legislation divided between a broad plurality (CS, II:iii, 147–148/372).

Similar to Madison, Rousseau agrees that enhanced numbers give rise to mob rule in one key sense: if deliberations concern any "particular" law. His belief is that the people must vote on general laws solely and that their enhanced numbers give rise to tumult if the laws are not kept general. It is not only that the general will "loses its natural rectitude when it is directed toward any individual, determinate object," but that those persons who are responsible for expressing this will become fractious and their decisionmaking "contentieuse" (CS, II:iv, 149/373). When the people assume the functions of the government they "introduce the most flagrant abuses of the wildest democracy."[28] Importantly, this is why the citizenry must never be allowed to vote on specific acts of civil or criminal legislation unrelated to the "conditions of the civil association." They may, on occasion, pass a tax or criminal code, for example, but they

---

[25] Hilail Gildin, *Rousseau's Social Contract: the Design of the Argument*, Chicago: The University of Chicago Press, 1983, 137.

[26] N.J.H. Dent, *A Rousseau Dictionary*, London: Blackwell, 1992, 206.

[27] Alfred Cobban, *Rousseau and the Modern State*, London: Allen and Unwin, 1934, 80.

[28] Cobban, *Rousseau and the Modern State*, 81. This complaint follows Hobbes' assertion that large deliberative assemblies ought to be kept from everyday politics and limited to the appointment of magistrates solely. Such a measure would prevent "suspicions and dissentions" rendering both large aristocracies as democracies the equal of monarchy, according to Hobbes. As the example of Venice demonstrates, when this is possible then the ills that befell early Athens and Rome are avoidable. See *Elements of Law*, II:v:8, 143.

must refrain from specific acts of lawmaking that reduce politics to a choice between "despotism or anarchy" (*CS*, 67/379; III:i, 167/397).

Considering that the bulk of the acts passed by state legislatures in the United States during the 1780s were particular acts of civil and criminal legislation it is, perhaps, historically significant to note that Hume, Madison and Rousseau share the common view that the "more multitudinous" an assembly, the more "passion" is the "slave of sophistry and declamation" (Federalist No. 58, 424–425). This said, arguably, where the latter breaks with his Anglo-American counterparts is in his belief that this vice is universal or true for "all numerous assemblies, *however* composed" (my italics). Rousseau rejects this conclusion because he believes that a well-composed assembly need not be a slave to sophistry or declamation so long as the laws remain truly general. So long as this is the case then assembly size matters only at the level of large states, such as Poland, where political power was delegated. In contrast to a small well-ordered state, it is well-ordered *government* that must be kept exceedingly small. In the *Social Contract*, Rousseau recommends an elective aristocracy, in part, because its limited numbers help to ensure that "assemblies are more conveniently held [and] business is better discussed and acted upon in a more orderly and diligent manner" (*CS*, III:v, 175/407; *CP*, 128/907). Ideally, "it is the best and most natural order for the wisest to govern the multitude" and "devices must not be multiplied uselessly, nor must twenty thousand men do what one hundred well-chosen men can do still better" (*CS*, III:v, 175/407). Unlike the sovereign who is free to act, though, he believes that a sword of Damocles must hang over this elite. At risk of being replaced at any moment, the government or Prince is not only subject to periodic review at election time, such as the deputies to England's Commons, but to daily scrutiny by a popular referee that may vote it out of office without notice.

Deviating from the opinion of Montesquieu, Rousseau asserts that large populations and states, but not necessarily large assemblies, are what undermine liberty. He does not agree with his hero that mandates necessarily render popular participation in lawmaking obsolete. Rather, if a population expands too quickly communal ties may grow weak and the legislative power of each sovereign-member diminishes proportionally (*CS*, III:i, 167–168/397), but legislation is still possible. Just as thousands of Greeks could be "constantly assembled in the public square" (*CS*, III:xii, 189/425; III:xv, 193/430), Rousseau argues that it is possible for large assemblies to legislate well so long as their members avoid decisionmaking on particular matters.

Conversely, Montesquieu highlights the perils associated with any type of expansion in *Considerations on the Causes of the Greatness of the Romans and their Decline* and the *Sprit of the Laws*. He claims that big states, diffused territories, expansive populations and oversized constituencies are incompatible with self-governance because long-established communal bonds will soften. Republican institutions "can have a place only in a small state, where one can educate the general populace and raise a whole people like a family." It is "in the nature of a republic to have only a small territory; otherwise, it can scarcely continue to exist." Similar to Hobbes' description of Athens, Montesquieu believes that Rome fell because "the ambitious" turned its assemblies into "veritable conspiracies" where "their laws, and even themselves became chimerical things." In the years leading up to the collapse of the Republic, "the ambitious" were able to bring "entire cities and nations to Rome to disturb the voting or get themselves elected." Within the *Comitia*, "the anarchy was such that it was no longer possible to know whether the people had or had not adopted an ordinance."[29]

In the *Spirit of the Laws*, Montesquieu emphasizes that one of the "great drawbacks" of popular assemblies and "great advantages of representation" is that officials are better "able to discuss public

---

[29] Montesquieu, *The Spirit of the Laws*, trans. and ed. Anne Cohler, Basia Miller and Harold Stone, Cambridge and London: Cambridge University Press, 1989 [1748], I:vii, 38; I:xvi, 124; *Considerations on the Causes of the Greatness of the Romans and their Decline*, 1965 [1734], 93.

business." His belief is that mandates make popular participation in lawmaking unnecessary (*Spirit of the Laws*, I:vi, 159). Such indirect interference in lawmaking need not prove to be deleterious to liberty so long as the state is kept small. Representative government is tenable so long as those responsible for choosing delegates and issuing mandates remain virtuous and united. Like Montesquieu, later American Antifederalist thinkers expand upon this notion to argue that lawmaking benefits most from majorities that are able to capitalize upon the talents of people from divergent walks of life. Large legislatures are said to be more cognizant of the common good than smaller lawmaking bodies. The *Federal Farmer* argues, for example, that "in order to allow professional men, merchants, traders, farmers, mechanics, etc., to bring a just proportion of their best informed men respectively into the legislature, the representation must be considerably numerous" (*Federal Farmer*, Letter II, October 9, 1787).[30]

In the *Social Contract* Rousseau agrees with this idea but for reasons different from either Montesquieu or the *Federal Farmer*. Rejecting the Antifederalists' emphasis upon diversity, Rousseau's belief is that the general will can be most easily realized when the laws come "from all to apply to all." Although public knowledge or cognizance of the general will is not necessarily a variable of number ("what generalizes the will is not so much the number of votes as the common interest that unites them" (*CS*, II:iv, 149/374)) even though all must vote for the outcome to be valid, the greater the number of active voters, the better. The philosopher's belief is that "personal interest is always found in inverse relation to duty, and it increases as the association becomes narrower and the engagement less sacred – invincible proof that the most general will is also the most just, and the voice of the people is in fact the voice of God" (*EP*, 144/246). Here, the "most general will" refers to numbers expressly and it is a widening of the "association" that supplants "personal

---

[30] *Federal Farmer* in W.B. Allen and G. Lloyd, *The Essential Antifederalist*, New York: Rowman and Littlefield, 2002, 149–150.

interest" with duty. Rousseau believes the "common interest" to be a variable of number yet, unlike earlier thinkers, his view is that its force expands rather than shrinks with increases in size. The actualization of "the most general will" occurs when the greatest number of citizens participate in lawmaking; when the least number participates then the ascendancy of personal interest results in the *least* general will. When every citizen participates the legitimacy of the popular vote increases despite the fact that each individual's relative percentage of the actual vote decreases. Here, Rousseau concurs with Madison that the larger the size of a popular constituency the more likely that its collective interests will reflect the common good.[31]

According to the philosopher, it is not only that the "better constituted the State, the more public affairs dominate private ones in the minds of the Citizens" (*CS*, III:xv,192–193/429–430) or the lesser the number of voters the higher the risk of particularity creeping into the assembly, but the definition of a law presupposes a standard of voting by everybody. As I briefly discuss in Chapter 1, Rousseau's terminology makes express reference to size for "when an entire people enacts something concerning the entire people, it considers only itself" and "then the subject matter of the enactment is general like the will that enacts. It is this act that I call a law" (*CS*, II:vi, 153/379). More pointedly, his sovereign is said to be "composed of as many members as there are voices in the assembly" in which "the constant will of all of the members of the State is the general will, which makes them citizens and free" (*CS*, I:vi, 139/361; II:iv, 200/440). According to the philosopher, "every act of Sovereignty" demands "the simple right" to vote by every citizen be respected and the whole of the citizen-body be consulted to create a law.[32]

---

[31] *Federalist* No. 10
[32] Masters comments that "the requirement that laws have a general source precludes the 'formal exclusion' of the vote of any citizen – universal suffrage in the popular assemblies is necessary even though unanimity is not." Of this, Melzer also remarks that alienation must be to a single, unified will that is inclusive of everybody, "the sovereign body must be the 'whole community.'" This means that the subjects must necessarily be members of the

Similar to ancient Rome where "no Citizen was excluded from the right to vote" and "no law received sanction, no magistrate was elected except in the Comitia," Rousseau's own "model of all free peoples" is one in which the citizens of a small state are "truly sovereign by right and in fact" (CS, IV:iv, 207/449). Of this expression of sovereignty, he recommends that Corsica establish a government where "all the members of the State collaborate in the supreme authority, which, making all the people perfectly level, allows it to spread out over the whole surface of the Island and to populate it evenly everywhere" (PC, 128/907). The absence of such a right is a "work of feudal barbarity that causes its most numerous, and often healthiest part to be cut off from the body of the State" (CGP, VI, 185/973). Although it may be that only a fraction of the population actually attends meetings of the assembly, it would be more just or equitable if there were general lawmaking by the whole body of the people. In this regard, Rousseau believes that increases in the number of voters ought to produce increases in the number of citizens who will (analogous to Tocqueville's jurors) be "forced to act upon other principles" beyond self-interest (CS, I:viii, 141/364) and have their "common deliberations" assume a "character of equity" (CS, II:iv, 149/374). Whether it is truly the case that laws made by larger majorities are indeed better than those ratified by smaller bodies is a controversy in the twentieth-century literature on epistemic democracy and Condorcet's Jury Theorem,[33] but for Rousseau his system of justice presupposes that assemblies will be big.

body that commands them and, what is more, that this body must be a *whole*, with a single unanimous will. The subjects are not promising here to obey the mere majority but the "whole community." See R.D. Masters, *The Political Philosophy of Rousseau*, Princeton: Princeton University Press, 1968, 334; A.M. Melzer, *The Natural Goodness of Man: on the System of Rousseau's Thought*, Chicago: The University of Chicago Press, 1990, 152.

[33] According to Condorcet (1785), increases in the number of representatives make it more likely – rather than less likely – that the decisions of a majority will prove to be correct. This is said to be true only for epistemic democracies (such as Rousseau's) that deliberate upon a binary choice and only up to a certain number of representatives, but Condorcet's jury theorem challenges the blanket view that large legislatures will necessarily legislate any worse than smaller

Toward this end, the Genevan argues that the chief danger to liberty is not assemblies of "any character composed" but assemblies of poorly composed character. Public opinion is what matters most to the realization and preservation of political freedom and the people's aptitude for self-governance is a variable of well-composed character, above all else. In *Poland, Corsica* and, to a lesser extent, the *Social Contract* the weight that the philosopher places upon *moeurs* above sheer numbers is evident from the litany of Roman-style institutions that he proposes to engender civic virtue and corporate unity across the whole of society. It is also evident from his willingness to empower a majority in the high hundreds, thousands and even tens of thousands with the lofty responsibility of sovereign lawmaking after these institutions take root. How *large* this actual number ought to be, though, is never assigned a firm number.[34] In contrast to his republican predecessors and his

lawmaking bodies. As some recent scholars have argued, iterated decisionmaking by large majorities improves enough over time (by people learning from their mistakes) to compensate for any deficiencies when the majority grows too large. See Jeremy Waldron, *Law and Disagreement*, Oxford: Oxford University Press, 1999, 135; Bernard Grofman and Scott L. Feld, "Rousseau's General Will: A Condorcetian Perspective," *American Political Science Review*, 3 (82) June 1988: 567–576.

Taking Condorcet's argument a step further, Alexis de Tocqueville is famous for arguing that this increase in "wisdom and enlightenment" owing to high numbers also confers a measure of "moral authority" upon the majority. He writes that "the moral authority of the majority is partly based on the notion that there is more enlightenment and wisdom in a numerous assembly than a single man, and the number of legislators is more important than how they are chosen. It is the theory of equality applied to brains." Alexis de Tocqueville, *Democracy in America*, ed. J.P. Mayer, trans. George Lawrence, New York: Harper and Row, 1969, I:vii, 247.

[34] Rousseau emphasizes the need for his state to be large enough to secure itself against foreign adversaries and for all of the citizenry to participate in voting, yet not so large as to render self-rule entirely impractical. Richard Fralin is right that much of what the philosopher comments about "the appropriate size of the body politic suffers from the neglect of it," although, in my view, this neglect is not so great as to veil Rousseau's general emphasis upon high numbers. Fralin raises a number of questions about whether Rousseau truly believes that a large body politic living in a state sizable enough to defend itself can do without representatives. See Richard Fralin, *Rousseau and Representation: a Study of the Development of his Concept of Political Institutions*, New York: Columbia University Press, 1978, 119.

contemporaries' longstanding fear of oversized assemblies, he argues that high numbers need not pose an intractable risk to law-making if those of the "character of a Socrates" are kept Socratic by a wise lawgiver, censor and tribunes, among other tertiary bodies. The people need not resemble a rabble if their *manniérés, moeurs* and opinion are adequately maintained and preserved or, at the very least, shielded from vice.

Considering Rousseau's tempered view of the political risks posed by high numbers it is, perhaps, easy to appreciate why Madison finds himself compelled to equate lawmaking by a large US House of Representatives with mob-rule. Stressing the need for well-balanced over well-composed institutions, the author of *Federalist* No. 10 must necessarily overstate the dangers of legislative size in order to understate the benefits of virtue to a "considerably numerous" legislature.[35] His rejection of a politics of virtue (why representative government does not rely upon goodness) requires a prior argument for why size matters – but not in the positive sense that Rousseau (or his Antifederalist opponents) identifies. Instead, Madison argues that a constitution that is capable of balancing "ambition against ambition" will necessarily render representatives with the lofty character of a Socrates superfluous. Even when filled with the likes of a Socrates the memberships of large legislative majorities will still be mobs. Regardless of the structures of government or the rigors of selection of a highly qualified elective elite, large assemblies remain inherently tumultuous.

In a veiled reference to Rousseau and the future Jacobin leaders of the French Revolution, Madison rejects their shared faith in the possibility of popular unanimity, observing that "theoretic politicians" have "erroneously supposed, that by reducing

---

[35] Madison recognized this viewpoint would find an audience. He hoped to exploit a common prejudice against large legislatures in making his case for a central-ized federal government. As Terence Ball writes, "the Antifederalist arguments about size and scale" of both republican constituencies and legislatures was "a rhetorical red herring of Madison's own devising." See Ball, "A Republic, If You Can Keep It," in Terence Ball and J.G.A. Pocock, eds., *Conceptual Change and the Constitution*, Wichita: University Press of Kansas, 1988, 145.

mankind to a perfect equality in their political rights, they would, at the same time, be perfectly equalized and assimilated in their possessions, their opinions, and their passions" (*Fed.* No. 10, 66). Unlike the idealized peasants in Rousseau's romanticized state of nature or just *patrie*, political majorities in the real world are discordant and so "long as the reason of man continues fallible, and he is at liberty to exercise it, different opinions will be formed" (*Fed.* No. 10, 63).

Anticipating this criticism, Rousseau offers two justifications in the *Social Contract* for why he believes that great assemblies can legislate rationally. The first is that the threat of numbers can be mitigated through institutions well-ordered enough to make it possible to achieve a degree of homogeneity and social unity in which there are "no tangled and contradictory interests" (*CS*, IV:i, 198/437). The second justification is that the difficulties associated with high numbers need not undermine the order of the assembly.

The first view, at the center of the philosopher's theory of indivisible sovereignty, is that numbers are unproblematic because political majorities can be socialized in a way as to exhibit an amazing degree of unanimity. Under the guidance of wise institutions a citizenry can be made to recognize the general will and express it concretely by way of a silent vote. If there are no tangled interests then popular deliberations ought to be wholly uncontroversial declarations of a self-evident will.

Of this perfect identification, Bernard Manin writes that legislative deliberation is reduced to split-second decisionmaking because "Rousseau's individuals are already supposed to know what they want when they come to a public assembly to decide in common. They have already determined their will, so that any act of persuasion attempted by others could only taint their will and oppress it." What is "evident, simple, and luminous does not need to be *deliberated* in the strong sense of the term" and the philosopher is "able to identify deliberation with decision making and decision with self-evidence."[36] As I describe in Chapter 3, though, such uniformity does not preclude the possibility of arbitrary opinion creeping into the assembly and, owing to this danger, it is impossible to predict the outcome of the vote adequately. Ideally, citizens ought to be able to ratify the laws in perfect unanimity but this outcome is rare if not exceptional.

From this idiosyncratic reworking of the traditional view of deliberation it is possible to object that the historic problems associated with great assemblies do not exist in Rousseau's state only because there isn't any actual "deliberation" present, in any conventional sense of the term. Sovereign rule under the social compact might be said to be achievable only because citizens are structurally gagged during the vote; were they ever to be free to engage in meaningful, open debate about the agenda then their numbers would prove to be impossibly burdensome. This is the gist of Benjamin Constant's criticism of his fellow Genevan, that his predecessor "declared that sovereignty could not be alienated, delegated or represented. This ... meant in practice destroying the principle which he had just proclaimed."[37] Sovereignty is believed to be impossible by Constant because popular majorities are too numerous or too fractious to act and Rousseau deliberately veils or obfuscates this verity by ascribing a meaning to the term "deliberation" that is really its opposite: non-deliberation.[38]

Against this powerful charge it is possible to show that Rousseau does not proscribe speech or discussion so much as he believes that it

---

[36] Bernard Manin, "On Legitimacy and Political Deliberation," in *New French Thought*, Princeton: Princeton University Press, 1994, 190, 191.

[37] Benjamin Constant, *Principles of Politics* in *Political Writings*, trans. and ed. Biancamaria Fontana, Cambridge and London: Cambridge University Press, 1988 [1815], 178.

[38] This notion finds substance in Rousseau's remarks about the inadequacy of the French political vocabulary. He comments that *"To Deliberate, To Give and Opinion, To Vote*, are three very different things that the French do not distinguish enough. *To Deliberate* is to weigh the pro and the con; *To Give an Opinion* is to state one's advice and to give the reasons for it; *To Vote* is one's suffrage, when nothing is left to do but to collect the votes. On the first round one give's one's opinion; one votes on the last round" (*LEM*, VII, 253n/833n).

is gratuitous for a citizenry that is cognizant of the general will. To achieve this lofty goal, though, he argues that well-crafted institutions for the edifying of public *moeurs* and the strengthening of civic ties must exist and their force be adequately felt before the assembly convenes. When citizens truly share a common understanding and interest in the common good then deliberation should be uncontroversial and the worst dangers of free speech bypassed. Although, the philosopher considers this to be a fragile disposition and he characterizes what transpires prior to the vote as being more regulated in his just state than it would be for peasants choosing beneath a tree, it is his belief that persons who are cognizant of the general will shouldn't want to deliberate. Unsurprisingly, perhaps, such a silence does not mean that every vote will be unanimous under every circumstance[39] nor that voting must *always* be undermined whenever citizens speak out but, rather, only that greater discussion is indicative of a softening of each citizen's private identification with the public good. Such deliberations will usually be divisive and the "closer opinions come to obtaining unanimous support, the more dominant" is the general will during the vote (*CS*, IV:ii, 199/439).

Presumably, within a tiny state the size of a boisterous minority would be large without being so extensive as to obstruct the exercise of sovereignty. More than the salience of numbers, though, it is the flawed character of such a minority's deliberations that would be most politically relevant. Rousseau's awareness of this distinction is evident from the unusually high threshold that he applies to the passage of important sovereign Laws – proportional majority

---

[39] This is similar to Ripstein who believes that in the absence of unanimity the general will ought to be understood as "a variety of overlapping and sometimes conflicting principles, each of which has some claim on the community's allegiance. As new circumstances arise, these considerations may come into conflict, or fail to speak with a single voice. The members of the community must then decide which has a greater claim on them, both by considering their grounds for accepting them and the consequences of their extension." Arthur Ripstein, "The General Will," in Christopher Morris, ed., *The Social Contract Theorists*, Lanham and New York: Rowman and Littlefield, 1999, 12:227.

rule – unlike the mere "business matters" of the prince that can be decided by a simple majority. By proposing such a standard he exhibits confidence that a substantial percentage of voters will be able to achieve a high level of rational agreement. Between "unanimity and a tie there are several qualified majorities, at any of which the proportion can be established, according to the conditions and needs of the body politic." Of these, it is only those "more suited to the laws," as opposed to "business matters," that ought to be decided by according to a higher standard.[40] His belief is that

> two general maxims can serve to regulate these ratios. One that the more important and serious the deliberations, the closer the winning opinion should be to unanimity. The other, that the more speed the business at hand requires, the smaller the prescribed difference in the division of opinions should be. In deliberations that must be finished on the spot, a majority of a single vote should suffice. The first of these maxims appears more suited to laws; the second to business matters. However that may be, it is a combination of the two that establishes the proper ratio of the deciding majority.
>
> (CS, IV:ii, 201/441)

This necessarily high criterion for voting reveals that, between the two distant poles of perfect unanimity and imperfect majoritarianism, Rousseau believes that lawmaking will likely be the product of deliberation whenever the state recedes away from the ideal. Correspondingly, it is possible to show that deliberation, as it is defined traditionally, exerts a consequential role during the *drafting* of the laws of the *Social Contract*. Unlike the silence that ought

---

[40] Arthur M. Melzer stresses the importance of achieving unanimity to realize the general will. By itself, majority rule is insufficient. "Rousseau is not taking the absurd and dangerous view that the general will is the same thing as the majority will" and his "precise position on majority rule is this: what is guaranteed is not that the majority vote will express the general will but simply that it – and only it – is at least structurally inclined to do so." Melzer, *The Natural Goodness of Man*, 161, 170.

to accompany the sovereign vote the drafting of initiatives would be marked by the presence of speech. This can be witnessed from the philosopher's willingness to allow the people an unchecked role in the framing of the laws and, more pointedly, his guarantee of discussion by right. It is not only a liberty "to discuss" but also "to give an opinion, to make propositions, to analyze" that Rousseau includes in this right (CS, IV:I, 199/439; LEM, VII, 249/827–828) with the last one ("to analyze") implying a type of deliberation that might be said to correspond to the standard dictionary definition of the term. Presumably, this right of analysis and opinion allows for a contestation of ideas even if such a contest might prove to be infrequent. During the drafting of the laws it is not necessary that each of the people be completely in agreement regarding the intent or effect of every law equally but, as Manin describes with respect to the ratifying of the laws, only that each citizen knows "exactly what he wants, or more precisely, he already possesses the criteria for evaluation that will permit him to appraise all possible alternatives."[41]

With regard to the second reason why Rousseau believes that high numbers will not create insurmountable obstacles to rational lawmaking, it is his belief that even non-ideal assemblies are capable of exhibiting a measure of order. Although the philosopher is, perhaps, the West's harshest critic of representative government, in his Letters Written from the Mountain he praises Geneva's Conseil général for its ability to avoid stasis and factionalism. He writes that unlike the ancient Greeks and Romans who got "mixed up" in "private business," Geneva's "hundreds of naturally serious and cold men" maintained order principally by keeping to themselves (LEM, IX, 293/881; VII, 251/831). Although such a disposition is debilitating to robust and spirited citizenship it enhances stability and he recommends the searching out of a middle ground where "public order" and the "public good" can be combined easily. In Geneva "the public order of your general Council is the easiest thing in the world; let

---

[41] Manin, "On Legitimacy and Political Deliberation," 192.

them sincerely wish to establish it for the public good, then everything will be free there, and everything will take place there more tranquilly than today" (*LEM*, VII, 252/832). In his well-known rejection of Hobbes' equating of England's Parliamentary "behemoth" with Athens' Pnyx, Rousseau follows Harrington by citing England's Parliament as an example of an exceedingly large and stable assembly in the seventh of his *Lettres*.[42] Offering rare praise for British parliamentary rule, he instructs Geneva's *petit Conseil* to follow the example of Westminster where the homogeneity of members' interests made lawmaking not of a mob but "uncomplicated" and the "business of a family:"

> They complain about the lack of public order that reigns in the Parliament of England; and yet that body composed of more than seven hundred members, in which such great affairs are treated, in which so many interests clash, in which so many cabals are fomented, in which so many heads become overheated, in which each member has a right to speak, everything is done, everything is expedited, that great Monarchy goes along as usual.
>
> (*LEM, VII, 252/831*)

This description is especially striking when juxtaposed beside Mill's comment that the "chaos" and "confusion" of England's Commons evinces "the utter unfitness of our legislative machinery" (*Representative Government*, 277).[43] Such a disparity of perceptions

---

[42] James Harrington is the exception to this larger tradition. Like Rousseau, Harrington sees England's Parliament as being a model size. A "rightly ordered" assembly, according to Harrington, ought to be only slightly less in size than Britain's House of Lords (the world's largest chamber). With as many as "one thousand or more," he argues that the ideal assembly can be kept in check by a senate consisting of as many as 300 members. See *The Commonwealth of Oceana and A System of Politics*, ed. J.G.A. Pocock, Cambridge and London: Cambridge University Press, 1992 [1656], 279–280.

[43] Mill's view is that "the utter unfitness of our legislative machinery" is "making itself practically felt every year." Arguing that Parliament should "have no power to alter" legislation because "any government fit for a high state of civilization, would have as one of its fundamental elements a small body," he bases this opinion on England's similarity to Athens. Of this likeness, he proposes

is not explained by time alone and this incongruity illuminates why the earlier of the two authors does not adopt England's Parliament as a political model despite its orderliness. Like Mill, Rousseau's belief is that inside of an assembly in which "everything is expedited" chaos must still exist in the sense that "cabals are formed" and, owing to this vice, sovereign rule is not possible no matter *how* orderly the forum. Specifically, England's Parliament is to be rejected because it is already a mob owing to its character regardless of its number. Similar to Geneva's *Conseil général*, the stability of this grandest of English institutions stems solely from apathy and indifference to freedom rather than corporate unity and a love of liberty. Within such a politically depraved state citizens are free only at the moment that their vote is registered and once this twinkling disappears Parliament is delivered back into the hands of foreign usurpers.

Regardless of its size, such a poorly composed assembly can only be a rabble in the way that Darius means "to combine together to maladminister the public concerns" (*History*, LXXXII, 249) because its delegates neither seek nor are guided by a uniform conception of the common good. Whatever orderliness is to be found in such a congress does not arise from any institutional benefits of parliamentary or representative government, according to Rousseau, but owing to members' need to overcome their inherent diversity (and venality) to establish order. Unlike Carl Schmitt who ascribes this problem to the nature of parliamentarism itself, i.e. the inherent divisiveness of discussion, Rousseau does not conclude that democracy ought to be rejected but, rather, that parliamentary rule is illegitimate owing to the absence of any knowledgeable or uniform conception of the common good.

as a solution that Parliament be limited in the same manner as "the popular Ecclesia" for "the necessity of some provision corresponding to this was felt even in the Athenian Democracy" where laws "could only be made or altered by a different and less numerous body, the Nomothetae" (Mill, "Considerations on Representative Government," 277, 279, 280).

ROUSSEAU AND "JURISPRUDENTIAL UNEASE
ABOUT LEGISLATION"

"No political problem is less susceptible of a precise solution," according to Madison, "than that which relates to the number most convenient for a representative legislature" (*Fed.* LV, 400). As true as this statement appears, Rousseau's writings reveal that the precise solution to this problem turns upon whether one believes that numbers must necessarily impede lawmaking even if civic institutions are capable of preventing political majorities from becoming mobs. Unlike the consensus of republican thinkers upon whose margins he skirts, Rousseau is unique in his view that the deleterious effects of legislative size can be mitigated by, among other things, well-crafted civil institutions. Unlike Madison and others who reject qualitative distinctions between assemblies of any high number, he believes it is only in assemblies with "the character of a Socrates" that the danger of numbers can be evaded. Most importantly, any and everything else is "mere mob" whatever the number.

5 Enforcing the laws in Poland and Corsica

A frequently debated question in the scholarship on Rousseau's political theory centers on the intent behind his constitutional plans for Poland and Corsica. In the 1960s a number of distinguished commentators, such as Judith N. Shklar, William H. Blanchard and Jean Guéhenno concluded that Rousseau's utopianism in *Considerations on the Government of Poland* and his *Project for Corsica* was intentional and originated from, above all else, a desire for polemical social criticism above serious constitutional reform. Since this time more recent authors, such as Arthur M. Melzer, have articulately refined this thesis by arguing for the "realism" or non-utopianism of this type of social criticism, but very few authors today believe that Rousseau sought the actual constitutional reform of Poland or Corsica.[1]

[1] A.M. Melzer, *The Natural Goodness of Man: on the System of Rousseau's Thought*, Chicago: The University of Chicago Press, 1990, 253–282; those who believe that Rousseau was serious about change in Poland and Corsica rarely argue for this thesis. Those who broach the subject of utopianism in Rousseau's political thought usually restrict discussion to general statements concerning 1) the "realism" of his desire to instruct Europe morally, or 2) the philosopher's intentions overall or with respect to the *Social Contract* exclusively or 3) general statements about the practicality of Rousseau's political project overall. These statements are usually part of a grander elaboration of different and wider textual themes. For authors in the first category see Melzer, *The Natural Goodness of Man*; Peter Gay, *The Party of Humanity: Essays in the French Enlightenment*, New York: Alfred A. Knopf, 1964, 250–253; and John Plamenatz, *Man and Society*, vol. I, New York: McGraw-Hill, 1963, 364, 388, 391; Plamenatz arrives at a diametrically opposite conclusion to Shklar but does not offer specific reasons for why he believes these works are practical. In the third category see Richard Fralin's brief remarks in *Rousseau and Representation*, New York: Columbia University Press, 1978, 180; Robert Shaver and, to a much lesser extent, Grace Roosevelt offer the most extensive treatments of the constitutional reforms in *Poland* and *Corsica*. See Shaver's two essays, "Paris and Patriotism," *History of Political Thought*, XII (4) winter 1991, and "Rousseau and Recognition," *Social Theory and Practice*, XV (3) fall 1989; Grace G. Roosevelt, *Reading Rousseau in the Nuclear Age*, Philadelphia: Temple University Press, 1990, 133.

In an extended study Maurice Cranston writes, for example, that "the best [Rousseau] could suggest for Poles was to nurture a spirit of patriotism and modify their social and political system" but, at root, his advice "told the Poles as politely as possible that in view of their circumstances freedom was not an option for them." Rousseau "used the Polish case as an occasion to indict all modern Europeans, who he said lacked the patriotic spirit and the institutions that had made possible the great political achievements of the ancient Greeks, Romans, and Israelites."[2] In a similar fashion, James Miller concludes that Rousseau's "unfinished and unpublished practical political projects, like all of his previous political writing, fitfully charted the uncertain region between dream and reality, between impossible ideals and remote possibilities ... the treacheries of attempting in practice, to travel the path indicated by his thinking had virtually convinced him to abandon the attempt. The dangers of action were intolerable."[3] These interpretations echo Shklar's assertion that Rousseau "was a social critic ... and not a designer of plans for political reform," that "the pseudo-realism of his Polish plan, with its endless descriptions of the details of organization and ritual, make it the most visionary, pejoratively utopian, of his works."[4]

These twentieth-century commentators are part of a long line of authors reaching back to Edmund Burke who, two centuries

---

[2] Maurice Cranston, *The Solitary Self: Jean-Jacques Rousseau in Exile and Adversity*, Chicago: The University of Chicago Press, 1997, 177–178.

[3] James Miller, *Rousseau: Dreamer of Democracy*, New Haven and London: Yale University Press, 1984, 131. In a similar fashion, Jean Guéhenno writes that in *Poland* Rousseau "was carried away by his dreams, he was intoxicated with virtuousness and giving full vein to his eccentricity. He was inventing the republic as he had invented a new system of musical notation. He was building the new city with all the fanaticism of a priest and the fantasy of a backyard inventor, and showing himself to be a forerunner of both Robespierre and Fourier" (*Jean-Jacques Rousseau*, vol. II (1758–1778), ed. and trans. J. and D. Weightman, New York: Columbia University Press, 1966, 262).

[4] Judith N. Shklar, *Men and Citizens: A Study of Rousseau's Social Theory*, Cambridge and New York: Cambridge University Press, 1987 [1969], vii, 14–15; also see Patrizia Longo Heckle, *The Statue of Glaucus: Rousseau's Modern Quest For Authenticity*, New York: Peter Lang Publishing, 1991, 154; Ran Sigard, "Rousseau: Freedom, Utopia, Bondage," *Iyyun*, 32, Jan–Apr. 1983, 41–55.

prior, characterized Rousseau's social and political theory as, "on the whole ... so inapplicable to real life" that it is impossible to draw any practical political lessons or conclusions.[5] Together with Benjamin Constant, Burke is one of the most eloquent of voices in this circle who claim, among other things, that Rousseau's purpose for writing the *Social Contract, Poland* and *Corsica* is to educate a corrupt Europe. Many agree with Constant that Rousseau would have been appalled to actually witness these plans achieve fruition.[6] Reading through the litany of creative and fanciful reforms recommended for Poland, in particular, it is easy to understand the prevalence of this view when one considers how much Rousseau's reliance upon "ceremonies and games, of plaques and insignia to impress the people ... reminds one of a clever god"[7] or – to cite one of the Genevan's defenders – his "national ceremonies and celebrations ... his praise of public games, spectacles, and solemnities ... may strike modern cosmopolitans as trivial."[8]

The popularity of this view aside, it is possible to argue that this ubiquitous criticism is unfounded to the extent that Rousseau's

[5] Edmund Burke, *Burke's Politics*, ed. R.S. Hoffman and Paul Levack, New York: Knopf, 1949, 389.

[6] Benjamin Constant writes that "Rousseau himself was ... horrorstruck at the immense social power he had ... created, he did not know into whose hands to commit such monstrous force, and he could find no other protection against the danger inseparable from such sovereignty, than an expedient which made its exercise impossible. He declared that sovereignty could not be alienated, delegated or represented. This was equivalent to declaring, in other words, that it could not be exercised." Constant, *Political Writings*, trans. and ed. Biancamaria Fontana, Cambridge: Cambridge University Press, 1988, 178; also see Stephen Holmes, *Benjamin Constant and the Origins of Modern Liberalism*, London and New Haven: Yale University Press, 1984, 91–92.

[7] The whole passage in Blanchard reads "it is the utopian quality in [Rousseau's] thinking that is likely to rouse the greatest resistance in the modern reader. When he speaks of remaking the human personality by remolding the form of government, of ceremonies and games, of plaques and insignia to impress the people, one is reminded of a clever god who manipulates men for their own good because they are ignorant and helpless to direct themselves ... Rousseau's principal value to his society was in his role as critic, the outsider who looked at the institutions of his day and found them wanting." William H. Blanchard, *Rousseau and the Spirit of Modern Revolt*, Ann Arbor: University of Michigan Press, 1967, 239.

[8] Roosevelt, *Rousseau in the Nuclear Age*, 133.

intent can be shown to be serious and his method comprehensible. More pointedly, it is possible to argue that the prescriptions for Poland and Corsica are grounded in a systematically consistent view of human nature that, despite its originality, is not entirely unpersuasive. These prescriptions demonstrate their author's desire for practicality in his search for a solution to the dangers that various *ennemis de l'opinion* pose to the laws and, critically, his willingness to satisfy this desire by means of a systematic methodology arising out of his larger social theory. Of the latter, to understand the substantive grounding that underpins this methodology it is useful to apprehend the formal process of law enforcement in Rousseau's state and, more narrowly, the policing of the laws in Poland and Corsica. By examining the philosopher's prescriptions for the government in the *Social Contract* and his recommendations for Poland and Corsica, it is possible to see how one of the most pervasive dangers to liberty can give rise to its own solution in a well-ordered state.

Contrary to the views of Guéhenno, Cranston and Shklar, it can be demonstrated that Rousseau is indeed serious about the constitutional reform for Poland and Corsica in the way that he describes. It may be the case that he is wrong or naïve in his observations and assumptions about human nature, but in his mind this is not true. As eccentric and archaic as his Romanesque proposals appear to modern eyes each can be said to provide evidence of the philosopher's desire for practicality and his willingness to satisfy this desire through carefully crafted reforms. Before making this argument it is, perhaps, useful to explore how he responded explicitly to the charge of utopianism leveled by critics in his own day.

RECONSIDERING ROUSSEAU'S INTENT FOR WRITING *POLAND* AND *CORSICA*

During the late eighteenth and early nineteenth-century, virtually all of the distinguished commentators on the *Social Contract* characterize its political theory as utopian. Although Voltaire and de Maistre are the most well-known of these critics, sympathizers such as Constant (who fretted over lumping Rousseau together with less thoughtful and well-intentioned thinkers, such as Mably) were equally critical in their appraisals of his pragmatism. During his lifetime Rousseau responded to these charges by vociferously condemning his attackers for deliberately misunderstanding his writings and misapprehending his intent. In a number of passages in his letters and writings he is explicit that his desire is to be practical even if such a goal appears to be far-fetched to the outside reader. Giving substance to this view in the eighth of his *Letters Written from the Mountain*, for example, he remarks that the *Social Contract* was intended to represent a clear break with earlier utopian tracts by thinkers such as More and Plato by exclaiming

> What! Sir; if I had only made a System, you can be sure that they [the authorities in Geneva] would have said nothing. They would have been content to relegate the *Social Contract* along with the *Republic* of Plato, *Utopia*, and *Severambes* into the land of the chimeras. But I depicted an existing object, and they wanted to change that object's face. My Book bore witness against the attack they were going to make. It is what they did not pardon me for.
>
> *(LEM, IX, 234/810)*

Unlike these earlier authors, Rousseau is explicit that he portrays something which already exists or something he hoped to exist one day. He writes *"if* I had only made a System," revealing his desire to create something real. Rather than being relegated "into the land of the chimeras," the *Social Contract* arouses public outrage because, unlike Plato's utopia, its unusual precepts conform to reality. Similarly, in the letter to Mirabeau from July 1767 that I cited earlier (Chapter 1), Rousseau rejects the physiocratic teachings of Mercier de la Rivière by remarking "You give too much weight to your calculations and not enough to the inclinations of the human heart and the play of the passions. Your system is very good for the people of Utopia; it is worthless for the children of Adam." This criticism of de la Rivière is significant not only because it clarifies what kind of politics the philosopher regards as impractical but, more significantly, because it defines his idea of a practical political program as one that takes account of "the human heart and the play of the passions." This notion, elaborated upon more fully in less popular writings like the *Letter to Alembert* and his letters to the Abbé of Saint Pierre, is unique in its challenge to more conventional conceptions of political pragmatism. Systems which ignore "the play of the passions" are the ones truly deserving of the utopian accusation because, to echo one of the Genevan's most famous lines, they fail at "taking men as they are and laws as they can be" (*CS*, I:i, 131/351).

Even if Rousseau considered the *Social Contract* to be a practical work one may retort that in the years leading up to the writing of *Poland* in 1771 the author's intentions changed. Such a shift may be apparent even if Rousseau didn't acknowledge in this privately commissioned work that civil laws banning opera, forbidding French dress or promoting Spartan-type public exercises were, at the very least, questionable. This said, what is most striking is that, especially in *Poland*, Rousseau not only repeats his strident declaration from the eighth of his *Letters Written from the Mountain* but, pointedly, condemns critics who level such charges as "superficial." Chastising those who would discount his methodology he defends his proposals as a necessary support for the laws by asking how is it possible "to move hearts, and make the fatherland and laws loved? Shall I dare to say? With children's games; with institutions that are idle in the eyes of superficial men, but which form cherished habits and invincible attachments" (*CGP*, i, 171/955). Warning readers against "throwing ourselves into chimerical projects" (*CGP*, v, 183/970), he ultimately concludes his project with the summation: "however peculiar one might find them, I myself see nothing in them except what is well adapted to the human heart, what is good, what is practicable, especially in Poland" (*CGP*, xv, 240/1041). Unlike his criticism of de la Rivière, Rousseau's rebuke of "superficial men" poses an express challenge to those who would cursorily dismiss the seriousness of his intent. It demonstrates that *Poland* is intended to be a practical constitutional regimen even if some observers fail to appreciate its value. He reiterates this challenge in *Corsica* by asserting that, contrary to what some might believe, his prescriptions cannot be judged to be "impractical speculations" (PC, 153/936).

Each of these excerpts demonstrates Rousseau to be engaging in something beyond polemics. Arguably, identifying what this "something" is, though, is a less demonstrable matter. This difficulty is compounded by complications that flow from Poland's excessive size and heterogeneous population. *Poland* and *Corsica* may be written for the children of Adam yet suitable only for the people of utopia. This powerful criticism, material to the larger issue of the Genevan as a pragmatic theorist of constitutional reform, begs consideration of his reforms' effects as well as intent.

THE LOGICAL BASIS OF THE CONSTITUTIONAL REFORMS FOR POLAND AND CORSICA

Rousseau's reproach to "superficial men" springs from the Pollyannaish assumption that enlightened readers will be familiar with his proposals' underlying rationale. This supposition is naïve because such an underlying rationale, vital for making sense of his later political works, is not articulated expressly. Worse yet, the philosopher presumes that readers will recognize the intuitive rationality of his creative strictures and, in the absence of such intuition, be persuaded by arguments found in his earlier writings. But, as he observes sixteen years before he wrote *Poland*, such persuasion may be inadequate for "the ecstasies of tender hearts appear as so many chimeras to anyone who has not felt them. And the love of the fatherland, a hundred times more ardent and delightful than that of a mistress, likewise cannot be conceived except by being experienced" (EP, 151/255).

Whatever his frustrations, it remains the case that readers must turn to his *Letter to Alembert* and other early writings to be able to situate the social and educational regimens for Poland and Corsica within the framework of his larger social psychology. It is in these works, specifically, that one is able to appreciate the degree to which these regimens are grounded in a systematic and consistent view of human psychology. Alluded to only very briefly in *Corsica*, this psychology is such that "the great motive powers that make men act ... are sensual pleasure and vanity" (*PC*, 153/937; *LA*, 300/61–62), and it is this psychology that underpins Corsica's reforms as they channel such "motive powers" back toward the state. As the driving forces behind human action, man's passions and vanity offer pathways by which it is possible for "the genuine statesman" to extend "his respectable dominion over wills even more than over actions" (*EP*, 147/250).

At a very general level, readers first learn of these two "great motive powers" in the philosopher's speculations about original man's denaturing and in his dour introspections over the hegemonic rise of *l'opinion publique*. This belief flows from the thesis of the *Letter to Alembert* that opinion is the origin of *amour-propre* and that it alone decides the material objects of its expression (*LA*, 300/62; *Emile*, ii, 152/409; *PC*, 153/937). Opinion is an unruly queen that governs men's tastes and pleasures because "the rules on which they base their opinions are drawn only from their passions or their prejudices, which are the work of their passions" (*RPS*, viii, 71/1077).[9] *Amour-propre* is "the fruit of opinion" in the sense that the latter

---

[9] Rousseau asserts that "sociable man, always outside of himself, knows how to live only in the opinion of others; and it is, so to speak, from their judgment alone that he draws the sentiment of his own existence" (*DI*, II, 66/193; *LA*, 300/62; *E*, II, 80–86/304–311, *passim*). More than mere sentiment, persons think, behave and make preferences according to the whimsy and changing tastes of the crowd; individually and collectively each is unable to experience emotion, act on moral impulse or even comprehend first-order desires and preferences unimpeded by opinion's mediating influence (*LA*, 300/62). The "primary maxim of wisdom in this country" according to Julie's Lover, is that *"one must do as the others do"* and *"that is done, that is not done.* This is the supreme pronouncement" (*JNH*, II:xvii, 205/250). With this pronouncement popular opinion supplants autonomous, independent decision-making and each are ultimately rendered like "so many marionettes nailed to the same plank, or pulled by the same string" (*JNH*, II:xvii, 205/250).

defines the particular objects that persons find esteem-worthy and everything, including law, is subject to its vagaries. What is most consequential politically is that opinion affects citizens' emotional attachment to the laws by shaping judgments about what does or does not "flatter" their "noble pride" (*CGP*, iv, 182/970). As a pivotal source of honor in society, citizens decide to obey or disobey the laws solely according to its dictates (*LA*, 300–305/62–68; *CS*, IV: vii, 214–215/457–459).

Like all social beings, Poles and Corsicans desire popular esteem and, in Rousseau's view, this desire can be a source of strength or weakness to the state. This disposition poses an especially onerous challenge to statecraft because inside every arena where opinion and the laws may clash violence proves to be useless. Discussed briefly in Chapter 1, conventional methods of law enforcement are useless for controlling men over the long term because their "great motive powers" are impervious to reason and violence. Although "it may be easy … to make better laws" it is "impossible to make any that men's passions do not abuse" (*CGP*, I, 170/955). Liberty as the possibility of self-imposed law (*CS*, I, viii, 141–142/364–365) is a variable of opinion because it, rather than the sword, determines whether persons choose to obey law. All listen to opinion *first* in deciding which laws to obey. This is the essence of the philosopher's historically original claim that manners, morals and, above all, public opinion are "the genuine constitution of the State" and a factor upon which the success of all the laws depends (*CS*, II, xii, 164–165/394). No civil, political or criminal law is enforceable without its support.

In key respects, it is this obstructionism that explains why even the most pragmatic prescriptions in *Poland* and *Corsica* are only recommendations. These works merely suggest reforms that play upon socialized man's vulnerabilities but nothing is ever definite, complete or certain. All that is certain is that violence and reason are feckless and efforts to refashion or shape individuals' tastes and pleasures or, for that matter, prejudices by way of *amour-propre* can only sometimes succeed. Everything that Rousseau writes about public opinion demonstrates the concept to be too protean, mercurial or ever-changing to be controlled adequately. Pre-existing belief can be validated and reinforced but never indoctrinated. As Allan Bloom comments, "laws instituted in contradiction to public opinion must surely be disobeyed; thus, they not only fail to achieve their end but cause men to have contempt for law in general."[10] The danger for the laws is that "force having no power over minds" (*LA*, 300/62) individuals will *always* listen to opinion first. In *Corsica*, Rousseau cautions against this peril by remarking that fear is incapable of leading "men to do good" or ever awakening "a nation's activity" (*PC*, 153/937). This threat turns traditional law enforcement upside-down because "public opinion is not subject to constraint" and, as such, "there must be no vestige of constraint in the tribunal established to represent it" (*CS*, IV:vii, 215/459).

Taking bold pre-emptive steps, Rousseau moves to blunt opinion's danger to the laws by way of a series of reforms that, despite his critics, he describes as effective. These reforms are designed to bring *manières, moeurs* and opinion into conformity with the laws to ensure that the two never (or only very rarely) clash. Ironically, it is the idiosyncratic measures crafted to achieve this objective with the greatest efficacy that, by and large, have proven to be the most vulnerable to the charge of pseudo-realism. This is apparent with regard to the Romanesque recommendations for Poland that, over the last four decades, have been subject to especially harsh scrutiny. Of these proposals the "most visionary, pejoratively utopian" appear to be his recommendations for

1 parades and pageantry;
2 children's games; and
3 the ordering of the civil services according to "the eyes of the public."

---

[10] Jean-Jacques Rousseau, *Politics and the Arts, Letter to M. D'Alembert on the Theatre*, ed. and trans. Allan Bloom, Ithaca: Cornell University Press, 1960, xxxii.

All three of these proposals betray Rousseau's diminished faith that individuals can ever become virtuous on their own and, in agreement with Hobbes' and Locke's arguments for sovereignty, non-existent faith that men will ever voluntarily obey the natural laws in the absence of pervasive state intervention. Contrary to the view of American neo-conservative intellectuals, such as William Bennett and the late Gertrude Himmelfarb, Rousseau believes that there is little value in promoting the classical republican virtues on their own merits. Skeptical of their popular appeal he instead posits a series of creative initiatives to inculcate these virtues through natural and socialized susceptibilities common to all. With each of these proposals, Rousseau can be witnessed adhering to the psychological assumptions that inform his view of humankind and, critically, discerning a middle way between utopian faith and draconian punishments in his efforts at enforcement.

To come to terms with these assumptions it is useful to be reminded of how laws ought to be ordered in a well-governed state. At the outset, it should be noted that the recommendations that commentators traditionally consider the most utopian do not fall within the philosopher's formal definition of sovereign power. Rather, these laws are "particular" or decrees and how such measures are to be executed in his ideal state is remarkably similar to what is found in most states – by violence. Coercion or the threat of violence are the everyday means of policing and, despite the benefit of judicious institutions, recourse to the death penalty is occasionally necessary. Although Rousseau believes that violence and political legitimacy are inversely related he is not sanguine enough to believe that such ends or means can be mutually exclusive if the state is to survive. Appeal to the sword is what guarantees that obedience remains reciprocal. This said, critically, a key aspect of his preference for Rome over Sparta springs from Lycurgus' overemphasis on violence as a means to shaping morals. He praises Numa for being the true founder of Rome, as opposed to Romulus, because the former employed religion to guide the people as opposed to violence or relying on brute force solely. One must always remember that "bloodthirsty Legislators who, following Draco's example, know only how to menace and punish, resemble those bad tutors who bring up children only with a whip in their hand" (*FP*, IV:xv, 32/496).

According to Rousseau, the tertiary bodies that are responsible for implementing measures to regulate such things as primary and secondary education, recreational activities and the civil services are essential for helping to channel public opinion. Within the realm of government, one of the core functions of these bodies is to render violence by the state infrequent for "everything is irremediably lost once it is necessary to have recourse to the gallows and scaffold" (*FP*, IV: xxiii, 33/498). In the *Social Contract* this indirect support is most germane during the interim periods between formal meetings of the assembly. This timespan is pivotal to the success of basic law enforcement owing to the threat of private cabals, intrigues and partial associations that are able to undermine compliance. He argues that traditional methods of law enforcement will only have a chance of succeeding if such private interests are prevented from co-opting opinion or influencing the popular vote. There must be strictures for this *autorité d'un autre ordre* and, in *Poland*, these strictures fall under the domain of censorial committees that are responsible for "enunciating" opinion in a way that binds the state to public notions of honor. Their role is to enhance this congruence and, less openly, foster it by massaging people's perceptions about public honor expressed by way of the laws.

Playing upon individuals' susceptibility to *amour-propre*, good citizenship is made to be honorable by portraying certain laws in a flattering light. In *Poland*, it is through such an identification that the judgments of the "censorial or beneficent Committee" promote good citizenship in the same way that Rousseau believes the French Marshals ought to support the laws with regard to dueling in the *Letter to Alembert*. Of the latter, the purpose of censorship is to promulgate the laws in a manner that expands their force by exploiting *amour-propre*. "The use of seconds in duels, which became a passion in the kingdom of France, was abolished there by the following few words in the Edict of the King: *as for those who are so cowardly as to call upon seconds"* (*CS*, IV, vii, 215/459; *LA*, 300–305/62–65). In Poland, the role of the censorial committee is designed to promote good citizenship more broadly, by offering "praise and encouragement, based on good information they would make up precise lists of the private individuals of all stations whose conduct is worthy of honor and of recompense." Instrumentalizing man's greatest social passion, the committee ought to draw up "well-verified reports of the public voice" to enfranchise peasants and "ennoble certain cities collectively." In this way, Poland "would no longer be anything but a single body whose vigor and force would be increased at least tenfold" (*CGP*, XIII, 227–228/1025–1027; 229/1028).

Arguably, it is the astuteness of this view of human psychology with its emphasis upon individuals' sensitivity to spectacle that evinces the practicality of Rousseau's unconventional methods of law enforcement. For example, this realism can be said to be especially evident from his discerning use of grand pageantry and ceremonial in *Poland*. In *Poland*, the relationship between pageantry and the laws is, at first glance, difficult to appreciate and few commentators explore the value of the former to the latter in any detail (as Walter Bagehot does in the context of England). Prima facie, it is nearly impossible to imagine ornate ceremonial carriages, processional guards, roving bands of musicians or the flying of the royal colors to be a rampart for justice in any state. Each may elicit fleeting sentiment for the *patrie* but how such carefully orchestrated spectacle might engender universal support for the laws, specifically, is unclear. Ephemeral surges of pride may palpitate in the hearts of young conscripts, elderly veterans and other patriots but how such fervor could effect strict *garants contre toute entreprise injuste* or, in instances when arbitrary opinion directly contradicts the laws, satisfy the compact's need for universal obedience is vague. Divorced from Rousseau's assumptions about human nature, *Poland's* emphasis upon visual spectacle appears overwrought or, at best, unlikely to achieve the practical ends that would justify such an ornate display. By day scoundrels will wave the flag only to wait until nightfall to commit the next felonious deed.

This said, the link between obedience and spectacle becomes readily apparent when the latter is reconsidered with an eye to what Cesar Beccaria calls the "easy path of feelings." Beccaria, the Italian theorist and most eminent reformer of criminal law during the eighteenth century, praises Rousseau's efforts to erect a complex regulative program of enforcement and acknowledges his ideas regarding the relationship between law and opinion to be a profound discovery. Intimately familiar with his social theory, Beccaria considered the Genevan's explanation of the complicated relationship between emotion and obedience to be accurate and penetrating. In *On Crimes and Punishments* (1764), he echoes Rousseau's view that man's susceptibility to emotion, sensual stimuli and opinion is central to the laws' success. Concurring with the philosopher's suppositions about the "great motive powers that make men act," Beccaria alludes to Rousseau in his classic treatise, writing:

> A great man, who enlightens mankind even as it persecutes him, has shown in detail the principal precepts of an education which is truly useful to men ... it encourages virtue by the easy path of feelings ... rather than by the uncertain method of ordering them what to do, which gains only a feigned and fleeting obedience.[11]

And, in a fragment from another work:

> All customs depend upon opinion. In order to enforce the observance of a custom, the laws themselves must produce an opinion, for the man who is unpersuaded will always reckon on avoiding punishment, a reckoning which cannot be entirely

---

[11] Cesar Beccaria, *On Crimes and Punishments and other Writings*, ed. Richard Bellamy, trans. Richard Davies, Cambridge: Cambridge University Press, 1995, 110.

eliminated. Hence, most laws ought to be indirect to inspire customs which are desired and accepted by the subjects.[12]

Grand pageantry and spectacle are useful to the state because "the people's heart follows its eyes" and all are impressed "by the majesty of ceremony" (CGP, iii, 178/ 964). Hearts swell at the sight of cymbal-clashing, drum-beating marching bands, stately carriages and lavish floats. The intoxicating power of brilliant colors, animated tunes and other rich sensual delights overwhelms Poles to usher forth passions and emotions rooted deep in a distant and long-forgotten nature. An atavistic vestige of modern man's original self, this orchestrated visceral response is carefully managed to ensure that citizens' "love of the beautiful" is reprojected back toward the state and its laws and, by extension, toward the cause of liberty.[13] Describing the regiment of Saint-Gervais, for example, Rousseau writes that "the excellence of the tunes which animated them, the sound of the Drums, the glare of the torches, a certain military pomp in the midst of pleasure, all this created a very lively sensation that could not be experienced coldly" (LA, 351/123–124).[14]

[12] Beccaria, On Crimes and Punishments and Other Writings, 157.

[13] This "love of the beautiful is a sentiment as natural to the human heart as the love of self" (LA, 267/22). I am grateful to Yong Chai Hwee for reminding me about the authenticity of such a sentiment by those whose "love of self" is not what comes most naturally to the human heart. Joyous passion need not always be linked to self-love by all beings outside of the state of nature.

[14] The import of this childhood memory of the regiment of Saint-Gervais has been mined by Tracy B. Strong for its significance to the philosopher's concept of time. Although the identity of the dancing soldiers was only knowable from their dance (being temporally dislocated in the same way as the general will), Rousseau remarks that "in spite of time and variety of experience" his memory of the dance continues until today. Owing to the "very lively sensation" that he experienced from "the sound of the Drums, the glare of the torches," among other things, his memory of this was able to transcend the temporal boundaries of the dance itself. In much the same way, the impressions of spectators who enjoy the "by the majesty of ceremony" should create memories that give support to the laws between the meetings of the assembly. Although the orchestrations behind these impressions are temporally circumscribed their non-cognitive memories are unlimited by time. A variable of the sensations they engender, the value of such orchestrations is to the future support for the laws. Rousseau writes that it in the end was impossible "to pick up the dance again" owing to the soldiers' drunkenness yet the memory of this "public

Similarly, school competitions should award prizes for excellence in knowledge of Poland and its laws and for recreational displays of fraternity, equality and civic virtue. Prizes for exams requiring knowledge of Polish towns, highways, history and customs are to be handed out to distinguish the best students in the eyes of elders (*CGP*, iv, 180–181/966–968). At an early age, such activities ought to accustom children "to regulation, to equality, to fraternity, to competition, to living in the eyes of their fellow citizens and to desiring public approval" (*CGP*, IV, 181/968). These games and competitions are designed to teach children early in life that the common good is the sole source of honor in society. Fostering an emotional attachment to the laws, they are intended to provide an object for feelings and sentiments that would otherwise find more pernicious outlets.

In Poland, the instrumental value of play and recreation is not always apparent because, in part, its purpose is only discernable when readers are aware of "the great motive powers that make men act." Rousseau believes that, unlike the young Emile, Polish youth will be inflamed by *amour-propre* at an early age and they will actively strive to satisfy this desire by competitions in which each is rewarded with the acclamation of elders and peers. Ideally, children will grow to love the *patrie* because each associates acclamation and material rewards, such as colorful ribbons, trophies, medals and plaques, with the virtues that these competitions inspire.[15] Critically, it is with this aim in mind that he proposes an educational regimen to teach children to love "what is truly beautiful rather than what is deformed" (*EP*, 155/259).[16]

---

joy" "stayed with me" into adulthood (*LA*, 351/123–124). See Tracy B. Strong, *Jean-Jacques Rousseau: The Politics of the Ordinary*, Thousand Oaks and London: Sage Publications, 1994, 91.

[15] In this respect, the aesthetic qualities of different kinds of awards, i.e., their material properties, are also crucial for enhancing their appeal to children and link to the state. Ribbons, badges, trophy cups, etc., should arouse *amour-propre* by attracting the attention of others and informing observers about what each award represents.

[16] Similar to Rousseau's belief that the people always desire what is right but can sometimes be misled, the love of children is always directed to what is good

To achieve this end, instruction must start very early in life because individuals "must be taught as children" to become citizens (*EP*, 154/259). The primary object of such instruction ought to be the laws, "the only study suited to a good people." Citizens "must mediate on them constantly to love them, to observe them, even to correct them with the precautions that a subject of that importance requires, when the need for it is very pressing and well warranted" (*FP*, IV:vi, 29/492). It is this combination of emotional attachment and rational knowledge that makes for an inspiring and enlightened civic education; it is what serves to ensure, as I discuss in the previous chapter, that citizens are never men of poorly "composed character" or mobbish vices but, rather, a corporate body in which "public affairs always dominate" over private interests (*CS*, III:xv, 192–193/429–430).

With respect to pageantry and competitions, it is possible to show that Rousseau's plans for Poland and Corsica really do take persons "as they are" to the extent that the author never grounds his proposals in a Smithian or Mandevillean-type faith that human desire will always serve the interests of the community. This is because children and adults may esteem what they perceive as honorable but they will not always identify this honor with the state or its laws. By awarding young children with ribbons, medals and plaques for excellence in learning of the laws, Rousseau recommends that Poland cultivate this psychological association in a way that brings Poles to "respect and cherish" the laws that "flatter" their "noble pride." By regulating sporting competitions, children's games and academic examinations, according to the Genevan, the *patrie* alone is able to determine the ends that children find esteem-worthy. Unlike inside of traditional monarchies or republics, Poles would not acquiesce passively before the artists, actors, journalists or self-empowering *philosophes* who seek to exploit them.

although it can sometimes be led astray. For this observation I am grateful to W. Gooby and T. Sweetnums.

Rousseau's fear of such exploitation reveals why, for example, such an apparently insignificant job as tax-collection in *Corsica* is, in his words, "the key to our political Government" (*PC*, 152/935). Recapitulating a key criticism of the bourgeoisie, he warns that tax collectors possess the power to destroy society through their elevation of profit and "illicit abundance" above more salubrious ends. "Financiers by station" can color the virtues that citizens perceive as honorable in ways that "cover disinterestedness, simplicity of morals and all the virtues with disdain and opprobrium" (*PC*, 150/933). Ideally, adult citizens ought to be immune to such vices but the threat is especially great when the example that is being set before them comes from the state itself.

Together with grand spectacle and arranged recreations, the "public eye" (*les yeux du public*)[17] is another oddly idiosyncratic proposal that can only be made comprehensible when readers are cognizant of the psychological assumptions that underpin it. According to Rousseau, any and every social relation of any consequence to the community at large ought to be performed publicly and with full cognizance of others in mind. It is his belief that such transparency will reinforce salutary *moeurs* in the same way that *moeurs* are undermined by secrecy and, more concretely, such transparency ought to be manifest during the electing of senators, deputies and magistrates in Poland (*CGP*, XII, 222/1019). Conversely, with secrecy "morals and honor are nothing" because each citizen "easily hiding his conduct from the public eye, shows himself only by his reputation and is esteemed only for his riches" (*LA*, 294/54). To prevent such an outcome Poles and Corsicans must be vigilant about ensuring that all of the possibilities or grounds for deceit and temptation are left barren.

---

[17] I translate this term as the singular "public eye" in English but an accurate translation of *"les yeux du public"* from the French ought to be plural (the "public's eye"). Similar to *"l'opinion publiques,"* the plurality of the original term reveals it to be an archaic predecessor to the rationalist Enlightenment definition of public opinion.

Arguably, of all of the recommendations for Poland it is the "public eye" that is the most consequential for ensuring that the *pouvoir suprême* and the *jugement du public* do not clash. The philosopher asserts that Poland's independence depends upon the openness of citizens' conduct and opacity endangers freedom by enervating the force of the laws. By and large, this is what occurs in unjust or illegitimate states in which men are able to veil their conduct from the public eye and be judged solely on artifice. To counter this danger, the "public eye" ought to foster a general respect for the laws through praise, honor and esteem in a way that is similar to the Genevan's women's *cercles* in which esteem, praise and shame promote good *manières*. At his most extreme, Rousseau asserts that criminals ought to be "viewed with horror by everybody," as was the case in Rome, where "public hate or esteem was a penalty or reward dispensed by Law" (*FP*, IV:xii, 31/495).

This role reveals the "public eye" to be the obverse side of the *Letter to Alembert*'s deleterious notion of "living in others." A medium for directing *manières* and *moeurs* through its power to confer or withhold public acclamation, this construct can be said to differ from "living-in-others" by its agency, methods and aims. Unlike the latter, the agency of the public eye is (indirectly by way of the laws) reflective of the will of the Polish sovereign rather than partial associations, sects or cliques that fill society. Under the laws' influence it reflects the common good of the general will exclusively rather than any particular will expressed by a single group, subgroup or individual. In Poland the exploitation of citizens' *amour-propre* by the state is an expression of the common good of the people who, by their mandate, dictate to the Prince and the censor the particular laws that shape opinion.

To reinforce this unofficial check, Rousseau suggests arranging magistracies hierarchically according to the public eye (in this case, popular judgments of merit) to ensure that every public official harmonizes his duties with the wider interests of the population. Poles should "make it so that all Citizens feel themselves incessantly under the public's eyes, that no one advances and succeeds except by public favor, that no position, no employment be filled except by the wish of the nation" (*CGP*, xii, 222/1019). Even more than the earlier measures, this recommendation is logical or comprehensible to the extent that it utilizes an incentive structure that guarantees procedurally that the objects and rewards for meritorious service always correspond. Exploiting Poles' sensitivity to *amour-propre*, "the eyes of the public" inform officials' behavior while remunerating it in the one currency that every socialized being desires most. As such, senators, deputies and other public servants will recognize how, over time, their private interests will be more pleasurable when they mirror the common good. Although such officials may find it easier to appear effective than to *be* so, Rousseau believes that few will remain inclined to keep up the charade over the long term. In a complex magisterial bureaucracy, such as Poland's government, the competition for promotion by way of public acclamation will simply be too great. Over the long term, public officers ought to feel greater esteem for giving honest renderings of their expertise and so much so that even the lowliest bureaucrat should experience a reduced sense of self for elevating private interest above the common weal.

CONTEMPORARY EXAMPLES OF SIMILAR-TYPE PROPOSALS AND PRACTICES IN EUROPE AND THE UNITED STATES

Each of these unconventional prescriptions can be asserted to be "well adapted to the human heart" to the degree that they anticipate similar-type measures existent in the contemporary world. Arguably, such measures can be demonstrated to be wedded to a social psychology that, if not unlike Rousseau's, is, at the very least, congruent with it.

Of all of the proposals above, perhaps, this is especially true with regard to state-sponsored *spéctacle*. From the dazzling computer-designed pyrotechnical extravaganza of the Fourth of July celebrations in the United States to Queen Elizabeth's Golden Jubilee,

these and other contemporary staged spectaculars are far more visu-
ally and aurally stimulating than anything ever dreamed possible
by Rousseau. Eliciting intense sensual and emotional pleasures by
way of their rich visual and aural impressions, such orchestrated
events are skillfully designed to redirect the excitement that audi-
ences experience while observing these shows back toward the state
through subconscious reminders of all of the good that the mother
country conveys. Writ small, these and other illustrious celebrations (e.g. the ceremonies of the World Cup, the old Soviet May Day
Parades) are perhaps more reminiscent of the evocative grand imagery of Rome under the Caesars than of Rousseau's modest proposals
for Poland and Corsica, but their purpose is analogous. By exploiting
man's susceptibility to pleasure and *amour-propre* this merging of
stagecraft *with* statecraft fosters powerful subconscious identifica-
tions with the *patrie*.

Less auspiciously, the larger Western tradition of acknowledging special citizens with public commendations can be shown to
replicate Rousseau's reforms for children's games and competitions
by honoring citizens in a very overt manner that casts the state
in a positive light. In contemporary Europe and the United States,
for example, such honorifics are usually conferred by governors,
mayors, police chiefs, fire marshals or other public dignitaries and
are not restricted solely to those citizens whose actions exemplify
extraordinary heroism. Rather, such plaques and medals are usually
given out to individuals who, in their capacity as citizens, risked
life and limb for the greater good. Oftentimes, such acts are purely
reflexive and originate from impulses far removed from the ancient
notion of republican *virtú*, but these well-publicized good deeds are
always publicized in an unambiguous manner that reinforces public support for the laws. Like the children's competitions in *Poland*,
such public celebrations reward citizens with the adulation of peers,
elders and the community at large.

Similarly, recent variations of Rousseau's controversial notion
of the "the eyes of the public" can be seen in the formal and informal

checks in place today to monitor US federal and state legislative candidates during elections. Similar to Rousseau's plan for Poland, these checks mandate that candidates explain how their private interests (and bulging bank accounts) are commensurate with the larger interests of their constituents. For example, public disclosure laws, such as those requiring candidates to publicize their earnings, often compel wealthier individuals to humble themselves by explaining how they can act as empathetic interpreters of the common good when their own private good, relative to the population, is unusually uncommon. In another analogy, the US Capitol Hill hearings on President Obama's multi-billion dollar stimulus package to salvage the US economy aptly demonstrated the degree to which public servants are, unlike ever before, under constant and intense public scrutiny as television, radio and the Internet give citizens a real-time "public eye." These twenty-four-hour media forums not only provide legislative and executive officials with a bully pulpit from which to grandstand but enforce compliance with the Rousseauian demands of an observant public. The power of this degree of scrutiny is evident in the late US Secretary of State Edmund S. Muskie's comment that "You're more clearly accountable [if] you're more visible ... I tend to do a better job if I'm visible and accountable ... I like the pressure."[18]

Rousseau would concur with Muskie that intense oversight by the public keeps government clean and, more importantly, its laws and practices in harmony with the spirit of the general will. Even the best state requires well-ordered mechanisms to maintain transparency. For the Genevan the problem of a "free" press is that such a medium, by definition, is exploitable, fractious and "particular." Unless the media possesses the means to accurately reflect the people back to themselves then it cannot be said to be truly transparent.

Surprisingly, as debased as much of the modern media is today, in a key sense it can be said to realize one critical function of

[18] *The New York Times*, March 27, 1996, B, 11.

Rousseau's concept of the "public eye," however: by providing a forum for social gossip, rumor or commentary that unintentionally mimics the eighteenth-century salons or women's *cercles*. More effective than its political scrutiny (at least in the decades since Watergate), the mass media today serves to reinforce morals by widely publicizing corrupt, immoral or licentious behavior. Although this medium is oftentimes criticized for inadvertently sanctioning licentious behavior by popularizing it (think "Girls Gone Wild!"), the deterrent effect on behavior owing to this exposure is often ignored. This deterrent, arguably, is more the outcome of the current state of *moeurs* than the state of the media. For some, even the worst ignominy is still a kind of fame. It is in this vein that the mayor of a city in Michigan a few years ago was able to persuade local businesses to sandblast graffiti off their exterior walls and sidewalks by posting flyers branding the worst-kept properties in the city the "Dump of the Month." A fairly common ploy used by local officials in municipalities across the world, in this particular case, it took just a month for walls and walk-ways to be scrubbed clean.

A less vivid example at the federal level is a television commercial run by the US Department of the Interior that targets the dangers of drinking and boating. The television spots close with the warning "Drinking and boating is not just illegal, its stupid." Analogous to labeling the use of seconds in dueling cowardly, perhaps, this form of persuasion can be argued to play on the vanity of those who boat to provide an indirect support for the laws; it is intended to make any violation synonymous with stupidity. Individuals ought to refrain from drinking and boating to avoid appearing stupid in "the eyes of others" and ultimately feeling humiliated. This is apt censorship, according to Rousseau: "wise applications" that "enunciate" popular sentiment in a way that adds support to the laws. Both this television spot and the "Dump of the Month" can be argued to be pragmatic because they successfully exploit psychological attributes common to modern man's socialized nature. Each play upon "the great motive powers that make men act" which are the fruit of opinion (*PC*, 153/937; *LA*, 300/61–62).

OPINION AS A SOURCE OF LIBERTY IN THE
IDEAL STATE

This chapter has sought to illuminate the non-rational side of Rousseau's political philosophy. Much has been written about the role of feeling, emotion and *amour-propre* in the Genevan's social theory, but much less with respect to their instrumental role in his just polity. Rousseau's thoughts on the great motivational forces behind human conduct demonstrate the ambitious proposals in *Poland* and *Corsica* to be "well adapted to the human heart" because each exploit citizens' sensitivity to the non-rational in ways that readers of these later writings sometimes miss. In this regard, Rousseau's declaration to the Parisian archbishop that everything he writes is "always with the same principles, always the same morality, the same belief, the same maxims, and if you will the same opinions" (*LCB*, 22/928) holds true as the "talent of reigning consists of nothing else" than making the laws "beloved" (*EP*, 147/250). Toward this end, what is most striking about his recommendations is not their superficiality but how accurately each conforms to a view of man that still resonates in our own day. *Poland*'s and *Corsica*'s reforms illustrate that vulnerabilities inherently destructive to liberty can offer potential pathways to its redemption; opinion can be a boon as well as a blight to liberty. As he writes in *Political Economy*, "although the government is not the master of the law, it is no small thing to be its guarantor and to dispose of a thousand ways of making it beloved. The talent of reigning consists of nothing else" (*EP*, 147/250).

6   Judging the laws/when legislation fails

Of all of the stages of lawmaking in the *Social Contract* that of judging or adjudicating the laws is undoubtedly the least familiar. It is not only that Rousseau says very little about how the laws are to be adjudicated in his just state but that very few of his readers examine this subject at any length in their voluminous treatments of his politics. This is true not only for the Genevan's most distinguished commentators writing at the beginning of the twentieth century but for more recent scholars as well. Explorations of the topic are extremely brief and superficial at best. Arthur M. Melzer, for example, writes only that "Rousseau does not establish a clear distinction or separation between the judicial and executive powers."[1] Similarly, decades earlier C.E. Vaughan remarks how in judging the laws "large discretion [is] in the hands of the Executive," a body "less liable to be blinded by ignorance – than the body of citizens, as a whole."[2] A few years later, Alfred Cobban comments that "Rousseau distinguishes and separates the executive, legislative and judicial functions clearly enough. He takes for granted the division of the magistrature between those exercising executive and judicial functions, indicating that the judicial function is to be separated from the legislative because it is concerned with particular acts." Based upon his observations of Geneva, Rousseau assumes, according to Cobban, "there is to be a separate class of judges, though preferring the classical idea of choosing these for their general merit from the whole body of citizens, rather than the modern practice of recruiting them exclusively among the class of

---

[1] A.M. Melzer, *The Natural Goodness of Man: on the System of Rousseau's Thought*, Chicago: The University of Chicago Press, 1990, 205.
[2] C.E. Vaughan, *The Political Writings of Jean-Jacques Rousseau*, vol. II, Cambridge: Cambridge University Press, 1915, 63.

legal experts."[3] Much more recently, Nadia Urbinati remarks briefly that in Rousseau's state "only the authority that makes decrees can be represented (the executive and the judiciary) without danger of 'denuding' the sovereign."[4]

Arguably, the reasons behind this dearth of scholarly commentary are better known than the topic itself. Of these reasons, the most obvious is the accepted view that Rousseau does not have a judiciary by any modern sense of the term. What he proposes is a sub-unit within the executive whose function is not to adjudicate any sovereign law but, rather, to interpret or judge its application to particular cases. Said to arise from the highly idiosyncratic view of justice in the *Social Contract*, this idea originates from the philosopher's belief that the meaning of the laws ought to be "fully evident" in a state that is truly well-governed. Ideally, judging or interpreting the sovereign laws, so to speak, ought to be identical with its *execution* when the will of the people is fully known. When each is aware of the general will, according to Rousseau, judging ought to be wholly uncontroversial and all that is necessary is that the laws be enforced. This view, given greatest expression in the *Social Contract*, explains why the philosopher's remarks are so parsimonious on the subject and why, other than the censor, the prince or government is the only tertiary body mentioned with respect to the laws' administration. Following Montesquieu's belief that the judiciary ought to be nothing but the mouthpiece for legislation in the *Spirit of the Laws*,[5] Rousseau is assumed to believe that juridical discretion must be "invisible and null." In the *Social Contract*, it is the transparency and indivisibility of the general will at all stages of legislation that appears to make this streamlining of the executive

---

[3] A. Cobban, *Rousseau and the Modern State*, London: Allen and Unwin, 1934, 81–82.

[4] N. Urbinati, *Representative Democracy: Principles and Genealogy*, Chicago and London: The University of Chicago Press, 2006, 74.

[5] Montesquieu, *The Spirit of the Laws*, trans. Anne Cohler, Basia Miller and Harold Stone, Cambridge and London: Cambridge University Press, 1989 [1748], XI:vi:158.

and judicial powers within a single body possible; it is the integrity of the popular will that renders any checks exercised by the people over the judiciary compatible with republican government.

For the most part, this traditional reading of how laws are to be judged in the *Social Contract* is accurate but it is possible to argue that Rousseau's considerations on the subject are more complex and even more problematic than appears from this conflation of executive and judicial functions. Although it is indeed correct that the philosopher does not believe that any court is required to adjudicate any sovereign law it can be asserted that it is his belief that such a body must exist to adjudicate the decrees passed by the government. Decrees, the specific legal acts that make up the bulk of the regulations in his state, are generally construed as being a kind of law that is passed by a parliament or congress of deputies (but as a part of the prince's executive powers). Problematically, this latter body must be allowed a wide berth of judicial discretion but one that is not so wide as to be contrary to the spirit of the general will. Critically, no single piece of legislation in Rousseau's state ought to be contrary to the will of the people in either word or spirit and a key aspect of the overall lawmaking process of the *Social Contract* concerns how both laws and decrees are to be made to be consistent.

JUDGING THE LAWS IN ROUSSEAU'S STATE

How are applications of the laws to be judged? According to the theory of the *Social Contract* it is impossible for the sovereign itself to adjudicate because it is incapable of judging "particular things" owing to its disposition toward generality. Foundationally, it can be asserted that the answer to this question is that the body chosen to judge applications of the law ought to do so in the same spirit as the body that legislates them: easily, transparently and unanimously. In any well-governed state the act of judging applications of the law is an act of government, exclusively, and the workings of this body ought to remain simple and harmoniously uncloudy. Because the "maxims" of the general will ought to be "clear and perspicuous" and the common good "everywhere fully evident" (*CS*, IV:i, 121/437) those who decide the laws ought to be undivided. The role of the government is only to enforce the sovereign laws and, far from being their "master or author," according to Rousseau, the government is "only their guarantor, administrator, and at most, interpreter" (*FP*, IV:i, 28/491) in a very limited sense. Each of these three functions of guarantor, administrator and interpreter is part of a seamless unity in which enforcement and adjudication are merged into a single executive act.

Unlike in Great Britain where the High Court serves as the interpreter of Acts of Parliament or in the United States where the Supreme Court reviews the constitutionality of acts of Congress, for example, it can be argued that in Rousseau's *patrie* juridical oversight exists *solely* with respect to the laws' application. Although the philosopher does not permit mediation of any sovereign law (with a capital "L") by judges he does believe that civil and criminal decrees, the bulk of the regulations in his state, must be decided by courts. This is the only judicial interference that is permissible in a just state because the presence of constitutional interpreters would divide sovereignty; such interpreters would themselves become sovereign over the laws. In such an event the presence of a court of judges would be indistinguishable from a traditional parliament of *représentans* owing to its particularity; it would be incapable of comprehending the general will owing to its lack of generality. Regardless of how wise or how well-intentioned a tribunal, it is always the case that a high court is incompatible with popular sovereignty because its judgments can never be reflective or knowledgeable of the general will; its decisions can never be as impartial or immediate as the people deciding for themselves.

To preserve this immediacy, Rousseau adheres to the teachings of his hero, Montesquieu, who characterizes the role of any court as being "invisible and null" in a well-governed state.[6] According

---

[6] Montesquieu, *Spirit of the Laws*, XI:vi:158.

to Montesquieu, judges ought to act only as "the mouth that pronounces the words of the law, inanimate beings who can moderate neither its force nor its rigor."[7] Only in those cases in which the law is unclear or ambiguous should those who are appointed to adjudicate be allowed to voice an opinion. For the vast majority of cases such interpreters' "judgments ought to be fixed to such a degree that they are never anything but a precise text of the law."[8] What this means for Rousseau's system is that the spirit of the general will ought to be evident in every judicial decision, no matter how trifling. Just as the "institution of the laws" is the prerogative of the sovereign, he is explicit that the "spirit of these laws" is that "which the government should follow in applying them" (CS, 158/263). Those who are empowered to judge serve as a conduit for the general will in their capacity as legal interpreters. When the general will is "clear and perspicuous" every judicial ruling will be "fully evident" and if this does not occur it is because the laws were poorly drafted. Unlike the transparency of the general will, "if the Law were clear enough, it would not constantly need new interpretations, nor new modifications if it were wise enough" (FP, IV:vii, 29/493).

One domain in which the law is never clear or wise enough is in the realm of morals, according to Rousseau. The problem is that even the best legislation is not able to establish an exact enough measurement to serve as a rule for magistrates in their capacity to judge morals. Owing to this inexactitude the government is forbidden from condemning individuals because of their moral beliefs. It is not only the edicts of the Church that should not interfere with private belief but also the laws of the state itself. Government can reinforce public morals by way of incentives but never impose penalties. For example, the censorship in *Poland* is empowered to praise good conduct and confer public honors but never to punish (CGP, XIII, 227–229/1025–1026). Years before he penned this short work, Rousseau explains in the *Discourse on Inequality* that in "matters

---

[7] Montesquieu, *Spirit of the Laws*, XI:vi:163.
[8] Montesquieu, *Spirit of the Laws*, XI:vi:158.

of morals – where the Law cannot establish an exact enough measurement to serve as a rule for the Magistrate – the law very wisely, in order not to leave the fate or rank of Citizens at his discretion, forbids him the judgment of persons, leaving him only that of Actions" (*DI, Note* XIX, 94–95/222). Of the former, it is solely "up to public esteem to establish the difference between evil and good men. The Magistrate is judge only of rigorous right" (*DI, Note* XIX, 95/222–223). Critically, it is up to popular judgment alone to interpret the meaning behind the presence or absence of praise for different types of public behavior.

With respect to the question of how "particular laws" (with a small "l") or decrees might be adjudicated Rousseau writes that "the Government is on a small scale what the body politic that contains it is on a large scale" and within this small scale there is "one according to the order of tribunals" (*CS*, III:i, 168–169/398).[9] As earlier scholars have noted, his repudiation of representation is a rejection of representative sovereignty expressly, rather than of representative government, and the civil and criminal decrees in a well-ordered state would likely be drafted and ratified by a traditional parliament. Ideally, this parliament would enjoy minimal interference by the sovereign because the latter should not involve itself with particular things, as the problems that plagued Roman governance attest. This said, hypothetically, owing to this freedom those persons who are appointed to judge particular laws might base their rulings upon past legal judgments and precedents as traditional courts would in lieu of a better alternative. But such a grounding is obviously problematic. Unlike the sovereign laws in which generality is the sole source of legitimacy it is possible to speculate that continuity would be the primary source of legitimacy for decrees. How well or how poorly each of these two loci of *generality* and *continuity* can be reconciled is debatable, though, considering that it is the government alone that exercises total control over decrees.

[9] "*l'ordre des tribunaux*."

Significantly, it can be argued that such enormous legal power is not exercised in a vacuum and the theory of the *Social Contract* hints at how these two seemingly irreconcilable entities may be brought into harmony. To achieve this end, however, one must never forget that "the first and most important maxim" is to "follow the general will in all matters" (*EP*, I, 145/247). For "as soon as it is a matter of fact or a particular right concerning a point that has not been regulated by a prior, general convention, the affair is in dispute" and "just as the legislator's first duty is to make the laws conform to the general will" so must the administration "be in conformity with the laws" (*CS*, II:iv, 149/373; *EP*, I, 147/250).[10]

Contrary to the conclusion of some readers, Rousseau does not believe that it is permissible for the government simply to "be just" to achieve these ends, as he describes in *Political Economy* seemingly. Rather, what is required is something wider: that magistrates "be just" *and* regularly consult with the sovereign as part of "two infallible rules" for interpreting the general will. Minimally,

[10] This idea is captured by a distinction that John Rawls makes between what he calls the "summary conception" and the "practice conception" of rules. Analogous to Rousseau's view of the hierarchical relationship between sovereign Laws and executive decrees, Rawls explains that under the practice conception of rules certain actions are rendered wholly incoherent beyond the structural rules that define them. For example, a player of the game of baseball cannot alter or change any particular application of the rules without undermining the game as a whole, according to Rawls. He explains that "to engage in a practice, to perform those actions specified by a practice, means to follow the appropriate rules. If one wants to do an action which a certain practice specifies then there is no way to do it except to follow the rules which define it. Therefore it doesn't make sense for a person to raise the question whether or not a rule of practice correctly applies to *his* case where the action he contemplates is a form of action defined by a practice." One can witness how the practice conception of rules is analogous to Rousseau's view of the relationship between Laws and decrees in the *Social Contract* by Rawls' example of property violations. When such a violation is said to occur one may be "punished for stealing, for trespassing" yet this charge necessarily "presupposes the institution of property. It is impossible to say what punishment is, or to describe a particular instance of it, without referring to offices, actions, and offenses specified by practices." See John Rawls, "Two Concepts of Rules," *The Philosophical Review*, 64, 1955, 26, 30. On this analogy between Rawls' view of rules and Rousseau's understanding of executive decrees see Tracy B. Strong, *Jean-Jacques Rousseau: The Politics of the Ordinary*, Thousand Oaks and London: Sage Publications, 1994, 99.

it is adequate to "be just" only to the extent that it is logistically impractical for "the whole nation" to meet during "each unforeseen event." More important is that "the spirit of the law" ought to "help in deciding cases that the law could not foresee" with the exception of controversies about the finer points of civil or criminal law.[11] As "source and supplement of the laws," the general will "should always be consulted when they are lacking" (*EP*, 147/250). Although final adjudicatory power must remain with the government, it is the people who guide this process informally (but never formally) by way of "prior, general conventions" or consultation when certainty is "lacking."

In the case of Geneva, as Rousseau notes in the *Letters Written from the Mountain*, when there is a controversy over competing interpretations of the laws than the literal arbiter ought to be the *Conseil général* while the *petit Conseil* exercises final decisionmaking power over the laws' application. It is "up to the equity of the Magistrate to fix their meaning in practice" but "this right does not at all go to the point of changing the literal sense of the laws." When

[11] Following the *Spirit of the Laws*, it is only during a constitutional controversy that Rousseau allows the people to interpret the meaning of its own laws. But they can never debate the finer points of any civil or criminal law because they would likely be legislating "particular laws" indirectly. Rousseau says that no citizen can be "judge of the risk to which the law wills that he be exposed" and that "condemnation of a Criminal is a particular act ... hence, this condemnation is not to be made by the Sovereign" (*CS*, II:v, 151/377). Such a function would also prove to be unwieldy or impractical for an entire people. Unlike constitutional legislation in which the number of laws can always be kept small, the civil and criminal codes must be longer but not so long that they cannot be committed to memory (*FP*, IV:vi, 29/492). Considering Rousseau's many regulations for Poland and Corsica, for example, it is easy to appreciate why the people as a whole is ill-suited for such an endeavor even if the body of the laws is not overly large.

Although, citizens cannot judge the laws in particular cases "with regard to the right to pardon or to exempt a guilty man from the penalty prescribed by the law and pronounced by the judge, this belongs only to one who is above the judge and the law – which is to say, to the Sovereign. Yet its right in this matter is not very clear and the cases in which it is applied are very rare" (*CS*, II:v, 151–152/377). Likewise, in his *Letters Written from the Mountain*, Rousseau writes that, at least in the case of Geneva, the arbiter of individual legal disputes ought to be magistrates who "fix" the laws' "meaning in practice," though divisive controversies ought to be decided by the *Conseil générale* (*LEM*, VIII, 277/861).

there is confusion the "good sense that pronounces is then found in the general Council" (*LEM*, VIII, 277/861).

Unlike the robed judges who hold court in poorly ordered states, those who sit in judgment in Rousseau's state must carry out their functions under the scrutiny of an observant public. As a part of the executive they must carry out their official duties under public scrutiny, well aware that those to whom they are accountable are knowledgeable of the general will. Every decision made by this body is rendered before the public eye (*les yeux du public*) and, more significantly, before one that can remove them from office in a blink. Of this "politicization" of the judiciary, which is only problematic in flawed political states (and, here, arguably, Rousseau appears at his most utopian), it can be asserted that it is citizens' cognizance of the general will and magistrates' fears over its consultation that substantively check governmental power. Not unlike the publicity that accompanies the civil services in Poland this openness is intended to popularize judging indirectly. Both as a matter of right and of fact, government is constrained by the general will indirectly and no magistracy is ever free to ignore the will of the people.

THE PEOPLE AS A CHECK UPON CIVIL
AND CRIMINAL LAW

Unlike this de facto check, Rousseau imposes two *de jure* constraints upon the potentially dangerous concentration of power in the hands of the government in the *Social Contract*. The first of these official checks emanates from the sovereign's formal control over the executive; the second from the character of those who fill the judiciary. Complementary, both of these constraints serve to ensure that particular acts of civil and criminal law remain in harmony with the tenets of the general will even if consultation by the people is infrequent. Each serves to guarantee that those who apply particular laws and issue decrees always do so in the same spirit in which the sovereign laws were created. What Rousseau wants to avoid is depriving any citizen of his liberty in the way that the English do,

JUDGING THE LAWS/WHEN LEGISLATION FAILS 155

restricting all political freedom to the ballot box. He wants to avoid a situation in which a people "thinks its free" but, in reality, "greatly deceives itself" merely because "it is a slave, it is nothing" (*CS*, III:xv, 192/430).

With respect to the first of these two checks, he emphasizes how the key question of "does it please the People to leave the administration in the hands of those who are currently responsible for it" (CS, III:xviii, 197/436) exerts a surveillance power over representatives that carries with it enormous political risks. His view is that such hands can never be dismissive of the popular will without fear of political retribution. Although the people may not be permitted to ratify any particular law by themselves, their influence will bear down upon the executive process indirectly because, among other things, the recurring nature of voting and elections will secure compliance. Considering that most of the civil and criminal laws or decrees are to be judged on a daily basis by a body other than the people the mere possibility of a "no" vote ought to exercise an authoritative check upon government's judicial functions.

According to some commentators, this power to replace the government is a purely formal restriction that, at least superficially, appears to be inordinately weak. Two ubiquitous criticisms are that citizens will not be able to replace the government because either they will be too close to it or elections will be too loose a constraint. In my opinion, the first of these criticisms was addressed earlier (Chapter 3) by way of my illustration of the psychological freedom exercised by Rousseau's sovereign. Beyond creating and preserving corporate unity, hegemonic conditioning by the lawgiver never usurps the "free vote of the people." Of the second, the apparent failure of elections to influence politicians' behavior, it can be asserted that although Rousseau believes that a "no" vote will be rare, such a possibility cannot be dismissed by politicians. Although the "established Government must never be touched until it becomes incompatible with the public good" this rule is merely a "maxim of politics and not a rule of right, and the State is no more compelled to leave the civil authority to its leaders than military authority to its generals" (*CS*, III:xviii, 196/435). If elections do not achieve this end effectively then the election laws need to be reformed in a way that enhances rather than diminishes the power of the people. Contrary to the view of Urbinati, Johnston and others,[12] Rousseau's wish is to suspend a popularly authoritative sword of Damocles over the heads of magistrates and to let its blade fall if required to reform "the conditions of the civil association."

Intriguingly, this express political threat is not unlike the implicit legal threat exercised by the people upon the sovereign ruler in chapters XXI and XXVI of *Leviathan*. Although the people do not possess juridical power over the particular laws in either the *Social Contract* or *Leviathan*, it is their ability to survey both that is most consequential. As a form of surveillance power, the popular vote in Rousseau's state can be said to mirror Hobbes' requirement that the laws be published and that subjects be able to sue the sovereign.[13]

---

[12] Urbinati finds it paradoxical that magistrates can act without popular supervision and are free to "overrule the sovereign" in Rousseau's state. Yet such a paradox does not exist. Each and every time that the sovereign assembles it is able to override all executive decisions by way of a repetitive vote. At all times the sovereign is capable of reforming and, in a different capacity, replacing the government at its discretion. Although such occurrences ought to be rare it is contrary to statecraft to be able to ignore such a sword of Damocles suspended above the heads of the executive power. See Urbinati, *Representative Democracy*, 85; Steven Johnston, *Encountering Tragedy: Rousseau and the Project of Democratic Order*, Ithaca: Cornell University Press, 1999, 87.

[13] I am indebted to Bernard Manin for this insight on Hobbes' rationale for the popular appeal of suing the sovereign in *Leviathan*. According to Manin, the suit itself is politically consequential irrespective of the verdict rendered. Hobbes writes "If a subject have a controversy with his sovereign (of debt, or of right of possession of lands or goods, or concerning any service required at his hands, or concerning any penalty, corporeal or pecuniary) grounded on a precedent law, he hath the same liberty to sue for his right as if it were against a subject, and before such judges as are appointed by the sovereign" (*Leviathan*, XXI:ixx, 143–144). Although, Rousseau's citizens cannot "sue" over a clash of legal precedents or reject any particular law, public scrutiny forces the government to recognize their power implicitly. In this respect, Hobbes' sovereign is even less constrained and yet "the subject hath the liberty to demand the hearing of his cause, and sentence according to that law." It does not matter whether or not such a hearing is to be staged publicly because, according to Hobbes, the people may "demand ... sentence according to that law." Regardless of the

Although the verdict wrought by any legal suit brought against the sovereign is unenforceable, according to Hobbes, the mere possibility of the lodging of a legal suit by the people serves as a quasi-democratic check against the imposing of unpopular decrees. Such legally sanctioned public scrutiny would exert a subtle yet unmistakable imprint on the everyday laws that guide how people express their freedom in society.

As Carl J. Friedrich remarks, it is the recurring nature of elections that ensures that representatives always remain accountable.[14] Unlike political systems in which officials are unanswerable to the people, in a democracy it is the desire or motivation for re-election that serves to guarantee that representatives be responsive to the popular will. This sensitivity to public opinion is vital to the laws' success and to statecraft generally because, in the absence of real-time checks capable of ensuring political accountability, elected officials must still adhere to the popular mandate out of a fear of retribution at the ballot box. According to Rousseau's theory, this outcome should not instill fear into those who judge in the same way that it ought to instill fear into those who risk the fate of Cromwell during the laws' drafting.[15] Rather, it should simply remind those

"pretense of his power," Hobbes' sovereign can be argued to be constrained to the extent that its cognizance of subjects' knowledge of past rulings and expectations of future ones tacitly affect its behavior.

[14] Carl J. Friedrich, *Constitutional Government and Democracy*, New York: Harper and Brothers, 1937, 263–266; also see B. Manin, *The Principles of Representative Government*, Cambridge: Cambridge University Press, 1997, 166–167, 175–183.

[15] Any proposal that is rejected by the majority is said to not reflect the general will and, by implication, the body that proposed it is seen as unaware of the general will (*CS*, VI:ii, 200–201/441). As great as the desire would be for an elected elite to try to foist their own special interests onto the majority, the enormous costs associated with failure at this task would be weighty. One can speculate that this weight would prove especially onerous considering that up until the vote *commissaires* would be aware that prejudice, sentiment and emotion sway public opinion unpredictably. Those who fail at such efforts must accept the political consequences that come with legislating without knowing the general will and these costs may be exacting and brutal. One indication of Rousseau's thinking in this regard is his aside that "Cromwell would have been condemned to hard labor by the people of Berne, and the Duc de Beaufort sentenced to the reformatory by the Genevans" (*CS*, IV:i, 198/438). Those *commissaires* who err

who judge that both the object *and* the source of the laws is somebody else. By exploiting the possibility of a negative vote the popular assembly ought to be able to keep the laws congruent with the general will even during the intervals between its scheduled meetings.

In the *Social Contract*, the possibility of a "no" vote can be described as a problematical de facto separation of powers between the government's executive and judicial functions to the degree that magistrates are unfree to interpret any law in its purely administrative capacity. On occasion, it is possible that the two functions of administrating and adjudicating can clash if a government that dutifully "follows the general will in everything" appoints judges whose decisions are made without due care. More problematically, there is also an issue with respect to any lag-time between the ratifying and executing of sovereign laws and the enacting of decrees. As one scholar has noted, "sovereignty does not exist over time, or even in time" but, rather, it is "like a work of art in the sense that it exists only in the present." Just as in the state of nature man "can never be sure of being the same for two moments in his life" (*MG*, I:ii, 77/282), during voting each discrete moment in time can be considered distinct to those that precede or follow it;[16] the general will is free to change its direction. In an often quoted passage from Book II of the *Social Contract*, Rousseau describes the general will as being temporally unbounded

repeatedly will, at best, be discharged and, at worst, suffer a terrible fate on the order of what Rousseau thought Cromwell deserved.

[16] Strong highlights how Rousseau's view of time defines his state because "political society is held to exist solely in the present tense." The inability of time to transcend its temporal location reveals why it is that representation is not possible. The "strictures that Rousseau places on the representation of sovereignty derive from the particular nontemporal quality of sovereignty. If something exists solely in the present, then its only existence derives from the activity that it requires of those who engage it. Sovereignty is thus like a work of art in the sense that it exists only in the present." Critically, it can be argued that it is this special sense that *also* explains why administration is an art form in Rousseau's state. But, the philosopher's unusual concept of time is problematic for a body that straddles two different temporal locations; one that acts and is evaluated at two discretely separate moments. See Strong, *Jean-Jacques Rousseau*, 91.

though it is not impossible for a private will to agree with the general will on a given point, it is impossible, at least, for this agreement to be lasting and unchanging ... The Sovereign may well say, "I currently want what a particular man wants, or at least what he says he wants." But it cannot say "What that man will want tomorrow, I shall still want," since it is absurd for the will to tie itself down for the future.

(CS, II:I, 145/368)

Critically, this passage calls attention to a paradox in Rousseau's theory owing to the time lag between the laws' ratification and the people's later judgments about the accuracy or competency of the laws' execution by the government. This paradox is that no matter how faithfully or expeditiously any law is applied it must always be carried out during a separate or subsequent moment in time. Worse yet, no matter how expeditiously the laws are executed those who assume this magisterial responsibility must be judged by their efforts in a different temporal space than the ratifying vote. Although continuity is usually the norm it poses a theoretical quandary in Rousseau's system that sovereign-members in the present are authorized to decide upon whether magistrates have administered laws in the *past* in accordance with the general will faithfully. Sovereign-members assume this function only after the convening of a second meeting of the assembly that is to be held on a different date.

As a solution, it can be asserted that the Genevan offers a procedural remedy to this temporal dilemma by requiring the sovereign to always vote on the administration of the government *prior to* any subsequent vote. Rousseau requires that the first two questions asked always pertain to the form and body of the executive rather than to the substance of any general law. This careful ordering can be argued to be material to the continuity and stability of governmental power by effectively forcing citizens to scrutinize how well (or unwell) the dictates of their previous will were actualized before any formal knowledge of their present-day will is made explicit. Rousseau compels sovereign-members to consider the activities of government solely in relation to a past rather than to a future will. Although the philosopher's belief is that all would "sense" changes to the general will prior to any subsequent convening of the assembly, all would not alter the form of the association or remove judges or magistrates based upon this "sense" without a publically expressed knowledge. Pivotally, this ordering of the vote is intended to avert a paradox in which the congruence between a law's passage and execution is not held to a single standard or definition of the general will.

In a different vein, there is also an accenting of the differences in character between those persons who are appointed to police and to adjudicate the laws in the *Social Contract*. Just as Rousseau lauds Rome's republic, where "no magistrate was elected except in the Comitia" (*CS*, IV:iv, 207/449)[17] and every magistrate was chosen for his "probity, enlightenment [and] experience" (*CS*, III:v, 175/408), it is his belief that "personal merit offers more important reasons for preference than does riches" (*CS*, III:v, 176/408). Those who are appointed to serve as judges would be an elite only to the extent that it is their natural differences, as opposed to those of birth, wealth or title, that matter most. Similar to those experts who participate in the framing of the laws, those who are responsible for judging will never be too distant an elite owing to a natural descriptive similarity to the people.

Arguably, one can speculate that Rousseau's judges would be qualitatively similar to the legislative *commissaires* who co-draft the laws yet be endowed with a different form of technical expertise. And unlike those who help to draft initiatives, any shared identity with the people would be of even more importance to judges owing to their interpretive power as it serves as a binding end-point to leg-islation. Judges would be aristocratic only in the sense of possess-ing a larger or unequal share of the qualities that are natural to the

---

[17] See H. Gildin, *Rousseau's Social Contract: the Design of the Argument*, Chicago: The University of Chicago Press, 1983, 110.

whole of the citizenry. Critically, it would be the natural virtues of this distinctive class that matter more than any differences based on wealth, privilege or title with regards to whether or not judicial rulings can be deemed consistent with the tenets of the general will.[18]

Beyond considerations about how the laws should be judged in Rousseau's just state, arguably, the second least examined question in his political theory concerns what happens when they fail. This topic, related to that of how the laws ought to be administered, is significant because of the long-term dangers posed to sovereignty by the government and, in a severe crisis, by a dictator. How liberty is to be preserved by these institutions and *from* them is controversial in light of the participatory character of Rousseau's *patrie* and the permanence of the threat of usurpation. The idea of suspending the laws is a notion that is wholly anathema to the spirit of the *Social Contract* and yet Rousseau considers the risks arising from such an act to be negligible or, at the very least, secondary to the greater perils that arise from a weak executive. This apparent incongruity casts a spotlight on the cumbersome status of emergency government in his just state and on participatory democracy more generally.

WHEN THE LAWS FAIL

What happens when the laws fail? Rousseau asserts that when morals decline perceptibly and the power of the prince expands beyond a certain limit then all is to be considered lost. His belief is that because of these twin threats the ultimate ruin of the state is an inevitability that can be slowed but never wholly prevented. This said, it is also his view that such potentially lethal dangers can be mitigated by way of the appointment of a dictator to prevent a political or military catastrophe from destroying the state. This latter option, especially, is something that the people ought never to be afraid to implement because the absence of preventative action is the worst danger of all; liberty cannot be preserved by timidity during a crisis. The solution

---

[18] Also see Cobban, *Rousseau and the Modern State*, 82.

of dictatorship is no more evil than the calamities that this body is appointed to redress and, like Machiavelli, Rousseau believes that fortune only "demonstrates her power" where "dikes and dams have not been made to contain her."[19]

Although the causes of such destruction are varied it is "the inflexibility of the laws," according to Rousseau, that prevents the people "from adapting to events" that ultimately brings about "the downfall of the State" (CS, IV:vi, 212/455). As Friedrich remarks, "constitutional law cannot anticipate every situation" and extraordinary crises are often enabled by the constitution itself. Coupled with this enabling is the "order and slowness of formalities" (CS, IV:vi, 212/455). Even when the laws remain wholly unfixed a tension exists between the orderliness of lawmaking and the vagaries of political life.[20] Similar to other republican thinkers, Rousseau follows Montesquieu in associating the democratic character of a law with the *slowness* that accompanies will-formation; slowness is a measure of the laws' republican character and it is only emergency decrees that ought to be frequent. When the state is tranquil there ought to be little reason for frequent meetings by assembly-members. Although, in principle, the people may assemble at will Rousseau does not believe that individuals will pass any new laws on a frequent basis. As I note earlier, it is only the government that is empowered with the authority to convene regular meetings of the assembly but the sovereign can self-convene during an emergency. Despite its freedom to do so, it will refrain from gathering at all if

---

[19] Niccolò Machiavelli, *The Prince*, trans. and intro. Harvey C. Mansfield, Chicago: The University of Chicago Press, 1998, 98–99.

[20] The presence of such a tension is generally taken for granted but, arguably, greater popular participation during a crisis might actually improve conditions. A contemporary example of such a lessening of tensions might be increased popular participation in the drafting of a law-code relating to the present-day war on terror. Enhanced participation in the drafting of such a law code might help to alleviate domestic tensions by helping to legitimize any unavoidable encroachments upon citizens' liberties. If it is possible during a crisis, the "democratizing" of emergency lawmaking might help to make individuals more willing to obey burdensome or invasive strictures over the long term.

change is unnecessary and the decisions of the government are consistent with the spirit of the general will.

In a unique aspect of his theory, Rousseau breaks with other republican thinkers in his emphasis upon the elongated time that is needed for will formation as opposed to deliberation. His view is that time is indispensable to the crystallizing of the general will but it is superfluous and a liability during the actual vote. Both the crystallizing and the exercise of the general will are inversely related temporally because what "requires only good sense to be perceived" does not require wide discussion and, when it occurs, is merely symptomatic of its division. He believes that resort to a dictator may be vital to protect the state from such a division or, worse yet, laws so odious as to place the state into immediate danger.

Dictatorship

According to Rousseau's critics, the revival of this anachronistic institution from classical Rome is counter-intuitively anti-democratic. For the theorist *"par excellence* of participatory democracy" any revival of the Caesars seems a strange choice indeed. As Clinton L. Rossiter remarks, "dictatorship is a phenomenon which has intrigued almost all ordinary readers of history and almost no students of law and politics," but "the conspicuous exceptions to this statement are those two great admirers of republican Rome, Machiavelli and Rousseau."[21] Likewise, John B. Noone wonders "why this article is part of the contract I can only guess."[22] If the travails of Roman history were not enough to prevent the dredging up of this most anti-democratic of experiments then surely Hobbes' warning about the risks posed to republics by Cromwellian-style military leaders should have done so. And yet Rousseau endorses such a homecoming. How can this be so?

---

[21] Clinton L. Rossiter, *Constitutional Dictatorship*, Princeton: Princeton University Press, 1948, 15.
[22] John B. Noone, *Rousseau's Social Contract*, London, 1980, 86.

Implicitly, at least, the answer that is given to this question in the *Social Contract* is that a temporary dictatorship is a safer option than any lasting or permanent expansion in governmental power. On a scale of risks the augmenting of a temporally and functionally unfixed governmental power poses the greatest threat to any possible return to popular rule. Inside of a well-ordered state the appeal to a dictator is not considered to be the worst of all dangers but, rather, a useful evil for staving off the worst of catastrophes. Following Roman custom, he construes this special appointment not as a remedy to any ongoing calamity but, rather, its preventative. It is only *ex post facto* to such a calamity that he opts for a strengthening of the executive by way of an expansion in magisterial power.[23] This said, the danger to sovereignty posed by a dictator is not as severe as may appear in Book IV:vi of the *Social Contract*. A number of somewhat veiled constitutional checks together with careful attention to the history of dictatorship in republican Rome evince the existence of structural impediments to the entrenchment of dictatorial power.

Of these checks, four are worthy of greater scrutiny: first, contrary to appearances, any resort to dictatorship would be exercised only to prevent a *total* collapse of the state. According to Rousseau, appeal to such an extreme measure would be permissible only for those crises of the highest order; its imposition would be not merely irregular but truly exceptional as "only the greatest dangers can counterbalance the danger of disturbing the public order, and one should never suspend the sacred power of the laws except when the salvation of the fatherland is at stake" (*CS*, IV:vi, 138/456). His belief

---

[23] Of this increase in magisterial power as an act of final resort, by removing certain limitations upon the government or augmenting the scope of its prerogative, "it is not the authority of the laws that is altered, but merely the form by which they are administered" (*CS*, IV:vi, 212–213/456). Unlike dictatorship, this expansion of the executive is permissible because the danger to sovereignty has already been realized and what is needed now is *praxis* to reverse the situation. This said, depending on the nature or extremity of the danger to be confronted, a suspension of the laws may prove to be redundant. In the gravest of all crises, such as those in which the people erred by not appointing a dictator earlier, usurpation may be at hand already.

is that "extreme evils make violent remedies necessary, and one must seek to cure them at any price" (*CGP*, IX, 205/998) but that such evils ought to be rare in a well-ordered state. Importantly, the historical trajectory of Rome's collapse reveals that many causes led to the Republic's demise and to the ascendancy of the Caesars.[24] Far more often than not, resort to a dictator did not result in an abuse of any extraordinary or extra-constitutional power. Of this stability, Karl Loewenstein explains that of the ninety actual instances of dictatorship in late Rome prior to its collapse, more than half were the result of the later Republic's earlier tendencies toward empire. Imperious militarism or "military ventures which not infrequently threatened its very existence"[25] accelerated its eventual demise. Despite the high frequency of dictatorship the supreme penal powers of the state remained in the hands of the people. In a passage that could have been lifted right out of the pages of Rousseau's political writings, Loewenstein remarks that

> in not a single instance of the ninety-odd dictatorships of the republican period did an abuse of powers occur. None of the dictators tried to perpetuate himself beyond the appointed term or attempted to pervert the office into the establishment of a régime personnel. In general, the dictator felt honor-bound to terminate his assignment as speedily as circumstances permitted ... It is highly to the credit of the Roman political organization and of the individuals entrusted with such vast powers that the institution throughout remained constitutional and at no time was used for an illegal rule. Where, in all history, is this record of constitutional legality equaled?[26]

Contrary to a number of traditional histories of the Republic's later history, Loewenstein's observations illuminate both the

---

[24] Karl Loewenstein, *The Governance of Rome*, The Hague: Martinus Nijhoff, 1973, 81.

[25] Loewenstein, *The Governance of Rome*, 81.

[26] Loewenstein, *The Governance of Rome*, 79–80.

legalism and republicanism of this institution's early incarnations. And it is striking that Rousseau, without the benefit of modern historical research, offers up such an astutely incisive reading of Roman history in his defense of emergency powers. Arguably, to a degree, Loewenstein's account[27] of the actual history of dictatorship in the Republic gives substance to the plausibility of Romanesque constitutional dictatorship within the *Social Contract*'s politico-sociological framework.[28]

Likewise, Rousseau believes that a highly selective vetting could serve as a check upon the abuse of discretionary power by any dictator. Owing to the salutary *moeurs* of the people, "there was no fear that a Dictator would abuse his authority or that he would attempt to keep it beyond his term" (*CS*, IV:vi, 139/456). Rather, "it is not the danger that it might be abused but the danger that it might be debased which prompts me to object to the indiscriminate use of this supreme magistracy in the earliest times" (*CS*, IV:vi, 39/456–457). In part, this is so because it is entrusted to the "worthiest person." This view by the philosopher is not entirely unfounded if one remembers that the civil services in his state are designed to ensure that only the best citizens are conferred with magisterial power. It is not only those individuals who exercise sovereign power who are subject to intensive institutional conditioning but also those within the executive and civil services who exercise power less directly. In many respects, it is these tertiary bodies that are the object of even greater and more intense civic education, as is the case with the reforms for Poland and Corsica. The exemplary individual who is appointed to serve as dictator when the *patrie* is under grave threat must be first an exemplary citizen.

Rousseau was acutely aware of the institutional failings of the late Republic and deliberately incorporated reforms into his

---

[27] Loewenstein, *The Governance of Rome*, 75–88; Rossiter, *Constitutional Dictatorship*, 15–28.

[28] Also see Carl J. Friedrich, "Law and Dictatorship in the *Contrat Social*," in *Annales de philosophie politique: Rousseau et la philosophie politique*, Paris: Presses Universitaires de France, 1965, 77–97.

system to guard against a similar outcome. The failings highlighted by Montesquieu, especially the rapaciousness of the ambitions of Rome's leaders and their unquenchable taste for vainglory and celebration, were to be guided and channeled back toward the good of the state in a virtuous system. He believes that any usurping of power by a dictator is not to be feared because those who are the "worthiest person" for this high office will revere the laws above all. Ideally, the private interests of such a lofty individual will be indistinguishable from the public good. The presence of this identification (and its public recognition) is the chief criterion that defines who is "worthiest" including a reverence or appreciation for law that, at least as a concept, is central to Rousseau's understanding of the common good.

In a different vein, the Genevan states that "whatever may be the manner in which this important commission is conferred, it is important that its duration be fixed to a very brief term which can never be extended" (*CS*, IV:vi, 140/458). Following Rome, he recommends a term-limit of six months. Bracketed within this short time span "the Dictator had only time enough to attend to the need that had got him elected, he had no time to dream of other projects" (*CS*, IV:vi, 140/458). This restriction, borrowed from Roman constitutional democracy, represents a far more restricted option than the more conventional alternative of *senatus consultum ultimum* by which the Senate could exercise such power in perpetuity. Critically, what gives the former measure substance is the inability of a candidate to appoint himself or extend his own term.

Although Rousseau believes that only "the worthiest person" ought to be selected for such a powerful position, it is also his belief that virtue alone is insufficient to prevent this extra-constitutional body from abusing its authority. Absolute power is capable of corrupting even the worthiest of men. What is more relevant are the institutional constraints that are imposed to ensure that this body has "no time to dream of other projects." By keeping the dictator to a fixed term of six months to a year, Rousseau is able to affect the psychology of whoever holds this formidable office. It is possible to restrict this body's mental time horizon and arrest any imperialistic "dreams" of empire of the order that, in the end, helped to undermine Rome.

Lastly, it is apparent that public opinion exerts an indirect bearing on the nature of the dictator's powers also. In a footnote, Rousseau asserts that Cicero "did not dare to appoint himself" to this high office (CS, IV:vi, 140/457) out of a fear of offending the people. This fear of offence was manifest, in part, because Cicero was too honorable a person to challenge public notions of honor on a question so close to people's hearts. At least implicitly, the philosopher appears to endorse the existence of a similar-type constraint developing as an inevitable consequence of political transparency. Unlike Montesquieu's belief that the gravity of certain crises may be so great that "a veil has to be drawn, for a moment, over liberty, as one hides the statues of the gods,"[29] this modern notion of arcana imperii or raison d'etat is absent from the theory of the Social Contract. Every action by the dictator is before the eyes of the people even when a veil is drawn over liberty. Similar to republican Rome where "the dictator felt honor-bound to terminate his assignment as speedily as circumstances permitted" owing to the weight of the judgments of the people, in Rousseau's state the dictator ought to be cognizant of such judgments and sensitive to any negative perceptions. The power of this informal yoke ought to complement rather than to impede the formal freedom at the basis of his mandate.

Dissolution of the compact

Less dramatic than the machinations to save the state are the machinations that precede its downfall. Emanating from the debauchery of morals and concomitant expansion of governmental power, the final death knell to the social compact is the substitution of a single private good or interest for the general will. Sovereign authority is replaced by executive power as the dissolution of morals necessitates

---

[29] Montesquieu, The Spirit of the Laws, XII:ixx, 204.

an increase in the coercive forces of the prince to maintain order. Imperceptible at first sight, the effects of this change are discernible as particular laws are repeatedly introduced and every vote becomes marked by the presence of lengthy and debilitating deliberations. Asking "what state can hope to endure forever?" Rousseau acknowledges the fragility of every *patrie* owing to the inevitable demise of *moeurs* and the corruption of legislation. One ought not "to flatter oneself with giving a solidity to the work of men that human things do not allow" (*CS*, III:xi, 188/424). Such human things lose their solidity because, unlike the general will, all human things are destructible. Nothing in men's hearts can remain changeless once it acquires physicality in their hands.

Quixotically, perhaps, the best account of this unraveling is not found in the *Social Contract* but in two much earlier writings, Hobbes' *Elements of Law* and *De Cive*.[30] In these works, Hobbes's detailed account of venal lawmaking inside of the English behemoth that ushered in Oliver Cromwell can be said to capture what legislation would look like during the twilight years of Rousseau's state when the laws no longer mirror the general will. In his colorful description of the chaotic and demagogic English Parliament Hobbes paints a frighteningly vivid portrait of democratic debauchery at its

[30] In my opinion, the twentieth-century author who bears Hobbes' *imprinteur* on this question the most expressly is the jurist and Nazi sympathizer Carl Schmitt who argues for a contemporary leviathan state to oppose the anarchy and gridlock of the 1920s and 1930s Weimar government. In a number of his writings, Schmitt imbues the chaos of the German Reichstag with many of the essential traits of democracy described in Hobbes' *The Elements of Law* and, at least by his reading, *Leviathan*. Rightly, Franz Neumann comments that Schmitt's understanding of Germany's political situation in the 1920s and 1930s is based upon a radical perversion of Hobbes' theory in *Leviathan*. Writing at the height of World War II, Neumann rebukes Schmitt's opportunistic use of *Leviathan* in lieu of the more appropriate model of the Englishman's *Behemoth* to describe German politics before and, critically, after Weimar's collapse (Neumann's addition). Unlike Hobbes's Commonwealth in which the "vestiges of the rule of law and of individual rights are preserved" in "*Behemoth* or the *Long Parliament* ... the English civil war of the seventeenth century, depicts a non-state, a chaos, a situation of lawlessness, disorder and anarchy." In Franz Neumann, *Behemoth: The Structure and Practice of National Socialism*, New York: Octagon Books, 1963 [1944], Introductory Note, 42.

very worst. Arguably, the collapse of the state is not something that Rousseau devotes a great amount of time to examining because he sees it as being unavoidable and less interesting owing to its inevitability. The same cannot be said for Hobbes who is scathingly critical of popular rule generally despite his tolerance for a plural sovereign in *Leviathan*.

Following Hobbes' description of Athens and the Long Parliament, this final and wholly destructive collapse would be marked by the emergence of interested debate in the sovereign assembly directed by those of greatest oratorical talent. During this time, a susceptibility by the people to demagoguery by orators, rhetoricians and other "flatterers" would bring about their ultimate downfall (*EL*, II:v:3, 140; II:ii:5, 120–121; *De Cive*, X:vii, 133–134; *Leviathan*, XIX:viii, 121). Hobbes writes that, exploiting the power of rhetoric, the "tongue of man is a trumpet of warre, and sedition" (*De Cive*, V:v, 67; *EL*, II:viii:12, 175) that is used to excite "the flame of the passions" leaving "understanding … never enlightened but dazzled" (*Leviathan*, XIX:v, 120). Inside of this ill body, "the favourites of an assembly are many" and "where many are to be satisfied, and always new ones, this cannot be done without the Subjects oppression" (*Leviathan*, XIX:viii, 121; *De Cive*, X:vi, 131–132). In such an oppressed condition those of greatest oratorical talent will seek to patronize family, friends and cronies and exhibit a total disregard of the common good (*De Cive*, X:vi, 131–132; *Leviathan*, XIX:viii, 121).

In Hobbes' writings, "glory" is similar to Rousseauian *amour-propre* in the form of a sensitivity to "the flattery of others." Anticipating the later thinker's criticisms of its effects (and Tocqueville's warnings about majority tyranny), Hobbes comments that "what is done by many, is commended by many" (*De Cive*, X:vii, 133–134) and power and prosperity "maketh men in love with themselves" (*History of the Peloponnesian War*, 12–13). Such a love renders assembly-members naturally prone to bad counsel because those who are inflamed by self-love do not want to be counseled by truths that might diminish their narcissistic pleasures. For "it is hard for any man to love that counsel which maketh him love himself the less" (*History of the Peloponnesian War*, 12–13), the end result being that assemblies will be dominated by flatterers who give the people only half of any truth or no truth at all. Moved by flattery, democrats will mistakenly construe such false acclamation and approbation for more tangible measurements of social, economic, political and, most dangerously, military power. "Tormented with perpetuall cares, suspicions, and dissentions" (*De Cive*, X:iii, n129) among a litany of other vices, popular rule will collapse into a power vacuum that can only be filled by delegating a broad range of legislative and executive functions to an elite.

Unlike Hobbes' description of Cromwell's rise, Rousseau argues in the *Social Contract* that there will be instances in which the servility of the people is so extreme that silence and even unanimity become the air of the state's last breath. For the truest mark of political decay is not a boisterously contentious or fractious public but an indolent unity (*CS*, IV:ii, 200/439). With such a rigor mortis things have moved beyond the politically salvageable point where "contradictions and debates arise and the best advice is not accepted without disputes." Rather, *l'unanimité revient* as servility and dependency replace expressions of autonomy in the votes of the people. In such a dire condition the state "continues to subsist only in an illusory and ineffectual form" as "the basest interest brazenly adopts the sacred name of the public good." The people are once again a unity but only in the form of collective bearers of a debauched *will-of-all* rather than a rationally indivisible common good. Consensus re-emerges as all rally around the particular interests of the few to pass "iniquitous decrees ... under the name of the Laws" (*CS*, IV:i, 199/438).

JUDGING THE LAWS/WHEN LEGISLATION FAILS
Of all of the stages of lawmaking in the *Social Contract* that of judging or interpreting the laws can be argued to be the least familiar. It is not only that Rousseau says very little about how the laws are

to be decided in his state but that there is no thematic exegesis of judicial decisionmaking anywhere in the *Social Contract*. Despite this lack of an organizing principle it is evident that such interference is permissible with respect to particular acts of legislation or decrees so long as all of the decisions rendered reflect the public spirit. Of this symmetry, the activity of judging can be shown to be a richer construct in Rousseau's political philosophy than what is sometimes assured. Careful attention is given to how decrees are to be made compatible with the Laws and, more broadly, how the activity of the government is to be kept accountable to the sovereign. Likewise, the philosopher's anticipatory Roman-style solution to the danger of crisis is evinced to be equally rich. Although this solution is coherent only within the context of the historical or constitutional model upon which it is based, it is, nevertheless, comprehensible. And when no similar-type model can be found upon which to prevent the inevitable demise of his state then resort to this final model is not incomprehensible.

Conclusion: Law and liberty

This book has sought to illuminate an important but opaque aspect of Rousseau's political thought: the relationship between the people and the laws or, more broadly, lawmaking and liberty in the theory of the *Social Contract*. In this book I have attempted to show that the role of citizens in lawmaking in the Genevan's state is more active and robust than many scholars conclude today. How the general will is made known is by law*making* as much as by what precedes or follows the popular vote because Rousseau recognizes important benefits to voting as a political activity. It is not his belief that an expert elite ought to be the locus of power in his *patrie* but, rather, the center of gravity ought always to be the people. In this respect, popular sovereignty is less the location of political authority than the vitality and assertiveness of its exercise. "Consultation" is what is most consequential to civil freedom as "it is through the legislative power" that "the State subsists" (*CS*, III:xi, 188/424; IV:I, 199/438). Toward this end, beyond relocating or reducing this popular power surreptitiously, Rousseau goes to extraordinary lengths to shelter its force from government's pincers for as long a time as possible; he protects and even enhances the power of the people beyond the formal vote in seminal ways. Significantly, the ultimate long-term futility of this constitutional endeavor does not diminish the ends toward which it is directed or make his efforts any less interesting to political scientists. Just the opposite.

More than anything else, the multi-staged regimen for "legislating" the general will is revealed to be a complex if somewhat multi-bodied process by which abstract freedom is given concrete expression in the *Social Contract*. This regimen can also be considered *historical* owing to the lawgiver's lengthy efforts at transforming men into citizens capable of self-rule and *procedural* as an expression of mutually facilitative rules and institutions for making self-legislation possible. Of the latter, the constitutional design by which the laws are created and maintained institutionally – when liberty is at its zenith, according to Rousseau – occurs only after the lawgiver's disappearance when the risks to the viability or survivability of the state are at their greatest. It is at this stage that Rousseau's polity may be described, so to speak, as crossing the Rubicon; it is the moment that political legitimacy and liberty are determined entirely by the transparency and competency of sovereign lawmaking.

As I quote at the beginning of the introduction, law is a "celestial voice that tells each citizen the precepts of public reason, and teaches him" to "not be in contradiction with himself" (*EP*, 146/248). It is Rousseau's belief that this celestial voice cannot be discovered outside of man's original condition or listened to inside of civil society without the aid of well-ordered political institutions. In their absence all that remains for individuals are the "murmurs despised by tyranny" that accompany the paradox of each person being simultaneously introspective and self-interested and yet dependent upon others for the satisfaction of his happiness in modern society (*E*, I, 39–41/248–250). Of this anomalous state, each individual is left beyond himself and perennially miserable from being "dependent upon persons rather than upon things." Owing to this dependency, according to Rousseau, human happiness is held hostage to serpentine opinion; each is inexorably bound to the fleeting, arbitrary and oftentimes situational approval of strangers that is not only a state of unfreedom but also confusion as "there is a great difference between the value opinion gives to things and the one they really have" (*JNH*, V:ii, 450/550). Men are deaf to the celestial voice that might instruct each person about how "to act according to the maxims of his own judgment and not to be in contradiction with himself."

Above all, it is a well-ordered society that prevents this contradiction from emerging. Individuals' ability to hear or listen to this celestial voice is the result (ideally) of a transparent political process that, in many ways, is less complex than the evolutionary psychological problems it is designed to address. To prevent *amour-propre* from undermining human autonomy or "authenticity," the laws must give expression to the general will and do so not only during the time of the vote but afterwards, by way of an inviolable check upon the civil and criminal laws. Toward this end, the traditional view of the philosopher's legislative cycle as being one of ratification or execution exclusively can be said to be overly simplistic. This is because both of these processes can be shown to be bracketed by less familiar considerations of agenda-setting and, with respect to the civil and criminal laws, adjudication in the *Social Contract*. Critically, public knowledge of the general will ought to be universally apparent inside of a well-ordered state but – unfortunately – the mechanics behind its actualization in the laws is not universally apparent in the scholarship on Rousseau. Arguably, much of this turbidity is an epiphenomenon of the mysterious appeal and aura that shrouds that most curious of ancient institutions, the lawgiver. Examining what happens to legislation after this body's departure to its "future glory" in "the passage of time" (*CS*, II:vii, 154/381), I have attempted in this book to shift the focus away from this founding construct to other less well-known aspects of the Genevan's legislative cycle. For the most part, my emphasis has been upon when lawmaking is the least constrained according to the theory of the *Social Contract*.

Of the various overt and covert constraints upon this activity, the burgeoning scholarly consensus that believes that the philosopher deliberately or surreptitiously diminishes the sovereign power of the people can be shown to be overstated. In no short measure this exaggeration can be argued to distort both the word and the spirit of the theory of the *Social Contract* by diminishing the salience of Rousseau's essential distinction between sovereignty and government by identifying, according to some commentators, the latter as the locus of political authority. In actuality, it is magisterial power rather than majority rule that is the most constrained in his state and this is why he regards the form of this power to be of negligible importance to sovereignty. Some types of government may be more or less suitable than others depending upon circumstances but this qualification pertains solely to the successful application of popular authority. Ideally, an elective aristocracy is most suitable, yet this regime-type may prove to be inappropriate depending upon differences of number or unity within a population. For Rousseau, the form of the government is less material than the form of the sovereign so long as there is an effective separation of powers. Similar to Hobbes and other modern natural rights theorists, the location of political sovereignty is what matters most and the issue of typology or other formal matters is decidedly secondary. Critically, at every stage of the legislative cycle inside of a just state the exercise of majority rule is institutionally protected despite a wide berth of magisterial control.

According to Rousseau, the definition of a "self-made law" is one in which the force of the popular will impacts upon the content of the civil and criminal decrees and the character of their adjudication despite the people's formal absence. Those persons who are responsible for enforcing such acts and passing final judgment over them are never wholly free or unaccountable. Although the people may not block their acts, their every decision must follow the spirit of the general will or they will find themselves voted out of office. There is no such thing as lifetime tenure for any office or position in Rousseau's state; those who are responsible for enacting, policing or interpreting the laws are never static or permanent office-holders.

A second theme of this book has been Rousseau's solution to the problem of how it is possible for laws to be effectively enacted when *l'opinion*, rather than the sword, is what matters most in the minds of the people. As I argue in Chapter 5, however, the origin of this question has its roots in the social psychology explicated in the *Second Discourse* and it informs the seemingly fanciful strictures behind the philosopher's constitutional recommendations for

Poland and Corsica. This psychology gives substance to the necessity of such strictures by evincing their rationality. The rigors of shaping opinion reveal how reforms that appear to be bizarrely tethered to "the uncertain region between dream and reality,"[1] as James Miller comments, are, in reality, part of a coherent, thoughtful and systematically articulated solution to opinion's unconventional threat to liberty. Better suited to the citizen-soldiers of ancient Sparta than to the bourgeoisie of modern Europe, Rousseau's archaic solution is designed to buttress the laws and, more widely, liberty by exposing the hidden chains laid beneath the garlands of flowers strewn by the *ennemis de l'opinion*. It is by regulating opinion that this yoke is supplanted by the general will. Critically, the ability of the state to influence opinion without any resort to violence is instrumental to Rousseau's larger project in liberty generally.

As a treatment of this influence both inside and outside of the state, I have attempted to elucidate the somewhat neglected non-rational side of Rousseau's political theory in this book. Arguably, much has been written about the role of feeling, emotion and *amour-propre* in his social theory but not enough about the inadequacy of rationalist interpretations of the *Social Contract*. Although it is indeed true that reason is vital to the ratifying of the laws it is also the case that emotion and *amour-propre* are pivotal to the laws' success. Long-term obedience derives from the heart rather than the head because esteem motivates individuals beyond logic or violence; honor is more germane than the sword. Any meaningful political voice by the people depends upon the effectiveness of seemingly immaterial or frivolous measures that give the laws a hidden force.

Although such a voice can neither enunciate nor articulate its words audibly without refinement by outsiders, it is the people's voice nonetheless. In this crucial respect, Rousseau's conceptually innovative institutions are not intended to usurp the formal

---

[1] James Miller, *Rousseau: Dreamer of Democracy*, New Haven: Yale University Press, 1984, 131.

principles of political right that legitimize his compact so much as to preserve them against meddling by any "partial" body that may wish to impose its will. It is the Genevan's brilliance as a political philosopher or, more correctly, Rousseau's originality as a legislator that gives such formal principles substance by demonstrating how republican statecraft can be benefit democratic freedom so long as those who reign are never enchained.

Select bibliography

Affeldt, Stephen G. "The Force of Freedom: Rousseau on Forcing to be Free," *Political Theory*, **27** (3) 1999: 299–333.

Baker, Keith M. *Inventing the French Revolution: Essays on French Political Culture in the Eighteenth Century*, Cambridge and London: Cambridge University Press, 1990.

Barber, Benjamin R. *Strong Democracy: Participatory Politics for a New Age*, Berkeley: University of California Press, 1985.

Barker, Ernest. *The Social Contract: Essays by Locke, Hume, Rousseau*, London: Oxford University Press, 1947.

Cassirer, Ernst. *The Question of Jean-Jacques Rousseau*, trans. P. Gay, New York and New Haven: Yale University Press, 1963 [1954].

Cobban, Alfred. *Rousseau and the Modern State*, London: Allen and Unwin, 1934.

Constant, Benjamin, *Political Writings*, trans. and ed. Biancamaria Fontana, Cambridge and London: Cambridge University Press, 1988.

Crocker, Lester. G. *Rousseau's Social Contract: an Interpretive Essay*, Cleveland: Case Western University Press, 1968.

Cullen, D.E. *Freedom in Rousseau's Political Philosophy*, De Kalb: Northern Illinois University Press, 1993.

Dent, N.J.H. *Rousseau: an Introduction to his Psychological, Social and Political Theory*, London: Blackwell, 1988.

Derathé, Robert. *Le Rationalisme de J.J. Rousseau*, Paris: Vrin, 1948.

Derathé, Robert. *Jean Jacques Rousseau et la Science Politique de son Temps,* Paris: Vrin, 1950.

Ellenburg, Stephen. *Rousseau's Political Philosophy: an Interpretation from Within*, Ithaca: Cornell University Press, 1976.

Fralin, Richard. *Rousseau and Representation: a Study of the Development of his Concept of Political Institutions*, New York: Columbia University Press, 1978.

Friedrich, Carl J. "Law and Dictatorship in the *Contrat Social*," in *Annales de philosophie politique: Rousseau et la philosophie politique*, Paris: Presses Universitaires de France, 1965, 77–97.

Ganochaud, Collete. *L'opinion publique chez Jean Jacques Rousseau*, Atelier, Reproduction Des These, Universite de Lille III, Lille, 1980.

Gildin, Hilail. *Rousseau's Social Contract: the Design of the Argument*, Chicago: The University of Chicago Press, 1983.

Grofman, Bernard and Feld, Scott L. "Rousseau's General Will: a Condorcetian Perspective," *American Political Science Review* **82**, June 1988: 567–576.

Guéhenno, Jean. *Jean-Jacques Rousseau*, vol. II (1758–1778), ed. and trans. J. and D. Weightman, New York: Columbia University Press, 1966.

Gunn, J.A.W. *Queen of the World: Opinion in the Public Life of France from the Renaissance to the Revolution*, Voltaire Foundation, Oxford: Alden Press, 1995.

Hendel, Charles W. *Jean-Jacques Rousseau: Moralist*, vols. I and II, Oxford: Oxford University Press, 1934.

Hobbes, Thomas. De Cive in *The English Works of Thomas Hobbes of Malmesbury*, ed. Sir W. Molesworth, vol. II, London: John Bohn, 1841.

Honig, Bonnie. "Between Decision and Deliberation: Political Paradox in Democratic Theory," *American Political Science Review*, **101** (1) February 2007: 1–17.

Johnston, Steven. *Encountering Tragedy: Rousseau and the Project of Democratic Order*, Ithaca: Cornell University Press, 1999.

Kaufman, Alexander. "Reason, Self-Legislation and Legitimacy: Conceptions of Freedom in the Political Thought of Rousseau and Kant," *Review of Politics*, **59** (1) 1997: 25–52.

Kelly, Christopher. "To Persuade Without Convincing," *American Journal of Political Science*, **31**, 1987.

Kelly, Christopher. *Rousseau As Author*, Chicago and London: The University of Chicago Press, 2003.

Leigh, R.A. "Liberte et autorite dans le *Contrat Social*," in *Jean Jacques Rousseau et son Œuvre: Problems et Recherches*, Paris, 1964.

Loewenstein, Karl. *The Governance of Rome*, The Hague: Martinus Nijhoff, 1973.

McCormick, John P. "Rousseau's Rome and the Repudiation of Populist Republicanism," *CRISPP: Critical Review of International Social and Political Philosophy*, **10** (1) March 2007: 3–27.

Machiavelli, Niccolo. *The Prince*, trans. and intro. Harvey C. Mansfield, Chicago: The University of Chicago Press, 1998.

Madison, J., Hamilton, A. and Jay, J. *The Federalist*, Pennsylvania: The Franklin Library, 1977 [1788].

Manin, Bernard. "On Legitimacy and Political Deliberation," in Mark Lilla, ed., *New French Thought*, Princeton: Princeton University Press, 1994.

Manin, Bernard. *The Principles of Representative Government*, Cambridge: Cambridge University Press, 1997.

Masters, Roger D. *The Political Philosophy of Rousseau*, Princeton: Princeton University Press, 1968.

Melzer, Arthur M. "Rousseau's Moral Realism: Replacing Natural Law with the General Will," *American Political Science Review* **77,** June 1983: 633–651.

Melzer, Arthur M. *The Natural Goodness of Man: on the System of Rousseau's Thought*, Chicago: The University of Chicago Press, 1990.

Mill, John Stuart. "Considerations on Representative Government," in *Three Essays*, Oxford: Oxford University Press, 1975 [1861].

Miller, James. *Rousseau: Dreamer of Democracy*, New Haven: Yale University Press, 1984.

Montesquieu, Charles Louis de Secondat. *Considerations on the Causes of the Greatness of the Romans and their Decline*, trans. and intro. David Lowenthal, New York: The Free Press, 1965 [1734].

Montesquieu, Charles Louis de Secondat. *The Spirit of the Laws*, trans. and ed. Anne Cohler, Basia Miller and Harold Stone, Cambridge and London: Cambridge University Press, 1989 [1748].

Mosca, Gaetano. *The Ruling Class*, trans. Hannah D. Kahn, New York and London: McGraw-Hill, 1939.

Noone, John B. *Rousseau's Social Contract*, Athens, GA: University of Georgia Press, 1980.

O'Hagen, Timothy. *Rousseau*, London and New York: Routledge, 1999.

Ozouf, Mona. "'Public Opinion' at the End of the Old Regime," *Journal of Modern History* **60**, suppl., September 1988: S4–S9.

Pateman, Carole. *Participation and Democratic Theory*, Cambridge: Cambridge University Press, 1970.

Pitkin, Hanna Fenichel. *The Concept of Representation*, Berkeley: University of California Press, 1967.

Putterman, Ethan. "Rousseau on Agenda-Setting and Majority Rule," *American Political Science Review* **97,** August 2003: 459–69.

Putterman, Ethan. "Rousseau on the People as Legislative Gatekeepers, Not Framers," *American Political Science Review*, **99,** February 2005: 145–151.

Qvortrup, Mads. *The Political Philosophy of Jean-Jacques Rousseau: the Impossibility of Reason*, Manchester and New York: Manchester University Press, 2003.

Ripstein, Arthur. "The General Will," in Christopher Morris, ed., *The Social Contract Theorists*, Lanham and New York: Rowman and Littlefield, 1999, 219–237.

Rosenblatt, Helena. *Rousseau and Geneva: from the First Discourse to the Social Contract*, 1749–1762, Cambridge: Cambridge University Press, 1997.

Rousseau, Jean Jacques. *Œuvres Complètes*, 5 vols, eds. B. Gagnebin and M. Raymond, Paris: Gallimard, Bibliotheque de la Pléiade, 1959–1995.

Sartori, Giovanni. *The Theory of Democracy Revisited*, Part II, Chatham: Chatham House, 1987.

Schumpeter, Joseph A. *Capitalism, Socialism and Democracy*, London: Allen and Unwin, 1943.

Schwartzberg, Melissa. "Rousseau on Fundamental Law," *Political Studies*, **51**, 2003: 387–403.

Scott, John T. "Rousseau's Anti-Agenda-Setting Agenda and Contemporary Democratic Theory," *American Political Science Review* **99,** February 2005: 137–144.

Shaver, Robert. "Paris and Patriotism," *History of Political Thought*, **XII** (4) Winter 1991.

Shklar, Judith. N., *Men and Citizens: a Study of Rousseau's Social Theory*, Cambridge and New York: Cambridge University Press, 1987 [1969].

Starobinski, Jean. *Jean-Jacques Rousseau: Transparency and Obstruction*, trans. Arthur Goldhammer, intro. Robert J. Morrissey, Chicago and London: The University of Chicago Press, 1988 [1971].

Strauss, L. "On the Intention of Rousseau," in M. Cranston and R.S. Peters, eds., *Hobbes and Rousseau*, New York, 1972.

Strong, Tracy B. *Jean-Jacques Rousseau: the Politics of the Ordinary*, Thousand Oaks and London: Sage Publications, 1994.

Trachtenberg, Zev M. *Making Citizens: Rousseau's Political Theory of Culture*, London: Routledge, 1993.

Tocqueville, Alexis de. *Democracy in America*, ed. J.P. Mayer, trans. George Lawrence, New York: Harper and Row, 1969.

Urbinati, Nadia. *Representative Democracy: Principles and Genealogy*, Chicago and London: The University of Chicago Press, 2006.

Vaughan, C.E. *The Political Writings of Jean-Jacques Rousseau*, Vol. I and II, Cambridge: Cambridge University Press, 1915.

Viroli, Maurizio. *Jean Jacques Rousseau and the Well-Ordered Society*, trans. Derek Hanson, Cambridge: Cambridge University Press, 1988.

Waldron, Jeremy. *Law and Disagreement*, Oxford: Oxford University Press, 1999.

Name index

Subject index

Numbers in bold indicate lengthier discussions